Who
Controls
the
Mass
Media?

Who Controls the Mass Media?

Popular Myths and Economic Realities

MARTIN H. SEIDEN

Basic Books, Inc., Publishers

NEW YORK

To Sam Herbach

Acknowledgments

In writing this book I have drawn upon the findings of over a decade of basic research and personal participation in the process of decision making, both for the government and for privately owned media. This book also draws upon the information provided me by executives (too numerous to mention) who gave liberally of their time to respond to my inquiries regarding details of their professional responsibilities.

A special debt of gratitude is due Martin Kessler, Vice President and Editorial Director of Basic Books for his patience and perserverance and to my wife, Rosalie, for her invaluable encouragement, without which this book would not have been possible.

Permission is acknowledged to reprint selected statistics and data from A. C. Nielsen Company, *Advertising Age*, *Ayer Newspaper Directory*, *Broadcasting Magazine*, *Colombia Journalism Review*, *Journalism Quarterly* and *Television Magazine*.

Contents

Who Controls the Mass Media?

I

Access to the American Mind

Fear of the Media

Each weekday morning America's 67 million households purchase nearly 26 million newspapers. In the evening they purchase another 37 million newspapers. At night 40 million households or about 60 percent of the nation, have their television sets turned on and about the same proportion listen to the radio at some time during the day, while eating breakfast, cleaning the house, or commuting to or from work. In effect, more than one person in every household in America is reached by the mass media every day and a majority of Americans are reached by more then one medium in the same day.

A veritable torrent of information, advertising and entertainment pours through the 1,800 daily newspapers, 5,000 AM and FM radio stations and 950 commercial and educational television stations serving the American audience. In addition to this formidable array of facilities that provide daily service there are in the United States 8,800 *weekly* newspapers and over 9,600 weekly, monthly, and quarterly magazines and journals.[1]

Only with the greatest difficulty can anyone in the United States avoid the mass media. Indeed, the average American is exposed to the messages of these media to a far greater extent than to formal education, organized religion, or political parties.

There seems to be a consensus that this extensive exposure to the mass media places it high on the list of social institutions that affect human behavior. One popular theory has gone so far as to assert that "the medium is the message," that it is the means rather than the content of communications that influences the audience.[2] The fact that such a notion is taken seriously reveals the strength of the underlying conviction—generally shared by government officials, politicians, social scientists, and (with considerable pride) by people in the profession of communicating—that there is something *intrinsically* powerful about mass communications. This implies a belief that the human psyche is malleable and that with the right formula or even simply with sufficient exposure to the media, audiences can be manipulated. Indeed, not only is this view encouraged by advertising agencies but also by a new profession of "media men" that has evolved in recent years whose purpose is the sale and merchandising of political candidates through the "proper" use of the mass media.

It is understandable in the light of these beliefs that the mass media are for many a source of anxiety, and for some a source of fear. This explains why the mass media are held responsible for so many of our social, political and even physical ills. Thus, political leaders blame the media when their popularity wanes, and as we shall see, the media are believed to bear a large part of the responsibility for the growth of crime in America's cities, for social unrest and racial rioting, for narcotics addiction, for children's reading disabilities and even for lung cancer and heart disease.

But is this true? Do the owners, their employees, and those who buy time and space in the media in fact possess the power over the audience which both they and their critics agree is inherent in mass communication?

The available evidence, as this book will show, does not support this view. Indeed the evidence shows that the reverse is the case. It is with the audience and not the media that the power resides. In the every-day, operational sense, the American audience influences the type of entertainment, consumer products and even the political programs, that are brought before it by the mass media. As we shall explore in some detail, the democratic character of America's mass media is a natural outgrowth of its economic structure. Our media system operates on the premise that the audience is the customer and those who own and use the system are salesmen. This relationship permeates the mass media, affecting its financing, the nature of its content, and even the character of political advocacy.

By constantly being polled, the audience determines the type of programming that is offered by television and radio. (Newspapers and magazines learn of consumer desires by their circulation figures.) Audience polls, as we shall see, also guide the design of political platforms, and the types of products marketed, including their packaging and even their names.

Because the audience's attention is so essential to the success of the system, its influence over the media is exercised in its day-to-day operation, rather than as some vague, intangible desire on the part of those who own, operate, or use the mass media.

Unfortunately, the inner workings of our mass communications system are not generally understood. The author has found that even those directly involved—members of the government's regulatory staff and employees of the media themselves—lack a clear picture of the system's more important aspects. Each knows the workings of his own sphere, but has only the vaguest notion of how the rest of the system operates. Those in advertising only vaguely comprehend the issues and rules surrounding station ownership, few newspaper people know about microwave interconnection, and most program syndicators don't know what the Federal Communications Commission (FCC) license renewal process involves. The FCC staff has almost no knowledge of how time-buyers operate and few television program producers understand the strategy of newspaper or magazine editing. Least informed of all, however, are the so-called opinion makers, the nation's political leaders, writers, and intellectuals.

Protecting the American Mind

One result of this ignorance is that policies have been set in motion which, though well intended, are based on fear and misconception. The forces of the government are being marshalled to contain, if not to subdue, the allegedly powerful media. Swept along in a state of near panic, Congress, in 1971, passed a bill that limited political expenditures for television advertising, even though the bulk of television exposure (not including news coverage) obtained by presidential candidates is provided by the networks without charge. The bill was vetoed. The *Political Campaign Spending Act*, which became law in 1972, reflects a more thoughtful attitude in that it encompasses more than just television.

But fear of the media, particularly television, runs deep and finds expression in our view of a wide range of issues. It has also given rise to an increasing number of attempts to confine the media's area of activity and to create countervailing forces to its freedom of action.

Thus, the government, in 1971, financed a $1 million study of the impact on our young people of the violence shown on television. Congress banned the broadcasting of cigarette commercials and is now investigating the relationship between the advertising of drugs and our narcotics problem. The courts have required that broadcasters accept *anti*-commercials. The FCC has limited the prime-time programming of the three national television networks to three of the four prime-time hours (7:00 P.M. - 11:00 P.M.), the Justice Department has filed suit to break up the television networks, while the White House has called for greater control by local television broadcasters over network news. At the same time broadcast licenses are being increasingly threatened by federal attempts to restructure the industry so that it will conform to the government's definition of socially responsible behavior.

All these acts—and we could point to many more—reflect the fear and hostility felt in some quarters toward the mass media. This hostility has even spilled over to those who serve in its front ranks. Thus in 1972-1973 over 30 journalists were the subject of court orders and a few actually went to jail for failure to reveal their sources of information or for publishing "stolen" information, as the Supreme Court stripped the journalist of his traditional immunity.[3] Clearly the pace of the assault on mass communications in America is quickening, and each succeeding proposal for government control is more radical than its predecessor.

A Glance at Reality

As we hope to show in more detail later on, many of the fears fueling this assault simply have no basis in fact. For example, the idea that with enough money the right media man can readily win public office for his client is inconsistent with the facts which show that in 14 out of 32 senatorial contests in 1970 the winner spent *less* than the loser, and among the relatively big spenders who won, most were incumbents. Furthermore, a detailed description of the techniques employed by a successful media man (see Chapter IV) reveal that it is the candidate who was influenced by the public and not the reverse. Neither heavy expenditures nor the wisest use of the mass media necessarily "molds" public opinion. More frequently than not, success follows from an accurate assessment of the public will.

What about the assumption that crime in the streets is somehow related to violence shown on television? The National Institute of Mental Health, the highly respected government research center, after spending much time and money investigating this allegation, could find no solid evidence linking the inordinate display of violent behavior shown on most children's television programs with the current high crime rate. It did not recommend controls over television.

These findings were similar to an earlier study on the role of comic books. Most important, they concur with the observed behavior of the vast majority of American youth. As we shall see in Chapter VII, young people, those who were raised on television and who at the time of the Vietnam war were in their teens and early twenties, were the group in America most outspoken in opposition to the violence in Vietnam. They were also in the vanguard in the early civil rights campaigns and among the most active in opposing sexual discrimination. Paradoxically, those who were at the time over thirty were generally indifferent to the social and political problems of the period and were suitably dubbed by the President the "silent majority." The over-thirty group, however, was exposed in its youth to radio programs and movies relatively free of the violence so common in the mass media today.

That is not to say that violence is a desirable form of entertainment, but rather that there is substantial evidence that indicates that exposure to it or to any subject is not necessarily a form of instruction nor does it necessarily condition the audience, however young, in such a way as to offset or replace the more fundamental influences of family, friends, and the school.

That the mass media lack an *intrinsic* power to influence the public is clear if we consider those whom they would influence. The American audience is not a homogeneous mass. It consists of many subaudiences. These include the different races, religions, and ethnic and national cultures in the United States, as well as individual differences in sex, age, education, wealth and local origin.

Because of this diversity, the American audience lives by many different value systems. This provides for a wide range of reactions to the same information. What will attract one group will alienate another.

The value systems that are unique to each subaudience have deep cultural and historical roots. They are not communicated, they are inculcated. This is done by family, friends, and school, not by speeches, dramatizations, or 30-second spot announcements. However, like potholes in the poorly paved road, value systems generally leave some areas unfilled. In these areas, the media can have some effect on the attitude of an audience toward a subject that, for this audience, is of secondary importance. It is at this level that most commercial products seek to influence the public.

But, for the same reason that the selection of a particular brand of soap, cereal, or toothpaste is a relatively unimportant matter for most people, it is also almost impossible to create a brand loyalty. A successful advertising campaign is one that succeeds in familiarizing the public with the product (strangers are seldom invited into one's home) and possibly generating some curiosity about the product's effectiveness (*new*, *improved*, and etc.). In effect, advertisers are pleaders not manipulators. And their impact, when there is one, is shortlived.

Even if they wanted to, there is evidence that the mass media cannot alter or effect deeprooted attitudes. The failure of anti-cigarette commercials on television and radio are a case in point. Even with a well advertised threat of excruciating death and testimonials by dying victims, cigarette sales have continued to increase.

Another dramatic example of the ineffectiveness of the mass media in shaping our fundamental attitudes is the failure of wartime propaganda. How many people still bear hostile feelings toward the Germans and Japanese after five years of vituperation by the mass media during the second world war? And with what ease have both the U.S. and China renounced their mutual suspicion of one another after decades of active hostility and—for China—decades of hostile anti-American propaganda. Is this an indication of the ease with which public opinion is molded? Or is it not an indication that public opinion was never molded at all?

Or take the question of race relations. The complete absence of blacks from commercials, news programming and dramatizations of everyday life, has only recently been rectified. Their absence, of course, had been a form of information. It told them and the white audience a great deal about the accepted position of blacks (and other nonwhites) in our social structure. But the media were not responsible for the past repression. Nor should they now be credited with leading the nation into the new era of greater racial equality.

The changing role of the blacks in mass communications followed rather than preceded the civil rights upheaval of the last decade. The black revolution in America and its acceptance by the white majority was not a product of mass communications, but of forces more fundamental to the formation of private and public attitudes. The causes lie much deeper than 30-second spot announcements or dramatizations on brotherhood. In racial matters, as elsewhere, the media merely acted as a mirror of society, not the "molder" of its opinions, as the cliché would have us believe.

Myths concerning the power of the media are a serious matter for they are diverting us from identifying and coping with the real causes of difficult social and political problems. They also tend to bring in the government as the public's protector against the purported dangers posed by the media. This is bringing about a change in the government's role from moderator to active participant in our communications system. And that, as we shall show, has serious long term political implications.

Can the Government Protect?

Under proper control, government can be an efficient provider of important social services. But without effective external control, its unbridled power becomes a public menace without parallel. The mass media, to the extent that they are independent of the government, are the government's principal adversary and therefore its principal external control. The American constitution, in its infinite wisdom, saw the press as an important countervailing force to government power and, through the First Amendment, in effect gave it an independence no less important than that of the Supreme Court.

Thus to call upon the government to control the mass media is to subvert the principal control placed over the government. A free "press" is the linchpin of the American political system. If it had had its way would the government have permitted such frank television reporting from Vietnam? Or would it have allowed the *Washington Post* to investigate and report on its findings in what later became known as the Watergate affair? These two issues alone raise serious questions regarding the effectiveness of the traditional checks and balances in our political system for neither the Congress nor the judiciary were equal to the task. This indicates the enormous importance of a free media as a partner in government.

No less important in evaluating the government's future role as a regulator of the mass media is its terrible record as a source of reliable information. In the past, Americans had been accustomed to expect from their government a high degree of reliability in its official announcements. Occasional scandals yes, but not the *official* release of blatantly false information or the concealment of information to which the public has a right. Unhappily, things have changed. Official concealment (and even falsehoods) have increased during the last two decades. The resulting tension between the media and the federal government has itself become news.

Erik Barnouw, a leading historian of mass communications, attributes the first really serious breach of the American tradition of free public access to information to the late Secretary of State, John Foster Dulles. In his book,

The Image Empire, he relates how in August 1955, the communist regime of Mao Tsetung declared itself willing to admit American newsmen in return for the admission of Chinese newsmen into the United States. Dulles refused. Indeed so stringent was the ban on information from China that when in defiance of the State Department, William Worthy, a reporter for the Baltimore *Afro-American*, went to China, Under Secretary of State Robert Murphy successfully prevailed on William Paley of CBS not to carry Worthy's shortwave news reports.[4]

For the next 15 years, the American people were compelled to rely on the State Department, itself poorly informed, for information relating to China. Our resulting ignorance of China had a good deal to do with the government's misreading of the situation in Vietnam. As the *New York Times* editorialized on the day before the final ceasefire in Vietnam, "the United States might not have gone into Vietnam had the depth of schism between the Soviet Union and China been clearly perceived."[5]

With increasing frequency, the federal government also adopted a policy of releasing information that was patently false. The Eisenhower administration denied that U-2 overflights ever took place until the Russians paraded Gary Powers, the U-2 pilot, before the world press. Similarly the Kennedy administration initially denied our involvement in the Bay of Pigs fiasco, and gave numerous contradictory responses for our involvement in Vietnam. And President Johnson provided the Congress with patently false information on the Gulf of Tonkin incident. Subsequent attempts to disguise military and political bungling became so blatant that the term "credibility gap," a euphemism for government lying, came into widespread use. Today, falsification and concealment of information have become commonplace in the executive branch of the government.

The Watergate affair revealed a new and sinister dimension to this problem, since it involved experienced attorneys and presidential confidants who willingly adopted, as standard operating procedure, the most nefarious techniques in the exercise of power.

For our purposes, two aspects of Watergate merit particular attention. First, the entire affair revolved around the attempt to control, create and alter information. In the modern world the sum and substance of power rests on the public's ability or inability to obtain access to accurate information. The audacious manner in which the White House staff sought to monopolize political power by manipulating and stealing information was a natural outgrowth of the passivity with which the public and the Congress accepted the earlier concealment and falsification of information by the Executive branch.

Watergate also underlined the importance of a privately controlled mass media. The initial revelations of the affair were not the work of the Justice Department or of any government agency, but of two staffers on the *Washington Post*. And unlike most Congressional hearings that go unpublicized, the mass media, particularly television, recognized the importance of these disclosures and brought them to the public's attention.

The more than 300 hours of televised hearings carried by the three commercial networks on a rotational basis cost them a combined total of $10 million in lost advertising revenue. (Interestingly, the Public Broadcasting Service attracted $1 million in donations through their coverage of these hearings). That the public wanted these hearings televised was determined by the audience surveys. They showed that on an average day 30 percent of the viewing audience tuned in to the hearings (the others chose to watch the other networks' routine fare). When it was over, only 15 percent of the nation had failed to see at least one session of the hearings.[6]

It is significant that all of the aforementioned examples of government misconduct, and not just the Watergate affair, were eventually brought into the open and disseminated by the mass media. This is no accident. Nor is it based on a unique American cultural trait favoring truthfulness. But it does reflect the economic fact that unlike any other major communications system, including the British and French, the American government does not (yet) have a part in the financial support of the mass media nor in the selection of the persons who are involved in its operation. The much maligned advertising dollar has, as we shall see, protected the mass media from government control as much as has the First Amendment.

Elitism in America

Unfortunately, there are many who regard mass communications as an excellent tool for educating the public and look upon its use for commercial ends—the appeal to the greatest number—as a waste of a national resource. The uplifting objectives which they would substitute for the present commercial objectives would, however, alienate the mass audience which attracts advertiser support. Inevitably the media would then become dependent on government support, and government support necessarily goes hand-in-hand with government control.

There is, however, more involved than the questions of economic support and lofty objectives. Implicit in the reformers' argument is a belief that they know what is best for others. In effect, they see themselves as latter-day churchmen in possession of a more sensitive moral conscience than the rest of their countrymen. To some extent this outlook has begun to influence professional journalists who in increasing number are being trained at universities rather than on the job. The new journalists are becoming, in effect, a lesser clergy, seeking to educate the public instead of keeping it informed. As a result, the distinction between "news" and "editorials" is beginning to fade.

It is essential for the health of the American political system that there be a continuous state of tension between the government and the media and that the sharp lines separating their interests be maintained. But this state of tension must be for the right reasons. It cannot be sustained if the professional journalists themselves tamper with the information flowing through the system. Constitutional guarantees notwithstanding this would hand the government a moral imperative to "interpret" its way into the inner workings of mass communication.

The Contest Has Begun

Unhappily, this process of erosion has already begun, especially in broadcasting. The threat to the present system is greatest here. Newspapers, magazines and books have never been regulated in the United States and therefore are one step removed from government control. In broadcasting, however, there is a well established regulatory tradition and it has taken substantial strides toward changing government regulation into government control.

Just one of several possible examples will indicate the extent of the government's aggressiveness. On January 23,

1969, a three-member majority of a four-member quorum of the FCC (which has seven members) held that the license of television station WHDH (Boston) would not be renewed and its channel would be given to a competing applicant because the licensee—who operated the station for over ten years— also owned a local newspaper (the *Boston Herald Traveler*) and the competing applicant did not. This ruling, which was well intended, (the idea being to increase the number of "voices" in the Boston market) wiped out a $50 million asset and placed the future of the *Boston Herald Traveler* in serious doubt since the newspaper lived off the profits of the television station. The newspaper, the second largest in Boston, has since discontinued operation.

With the best of intentions, the government effectively deprived the Boston public of a major source of information. Worse still, the majority of the Commissioners held that this principle of not allowing a licensee to own more than one medium in a market now applied to *all* future license renewal proceedings (a policy also advocated by the Justice Department). An estimated $3 billion in broadcasting assets were thus put in jeopardy.[7] This policy, it should be noted, was not the result of a social, political or economic analysis of America's cities or of the mass media. Nor was it a reaction to a local or regional problem, nor even to public complaints. Indeed, the reverse applied in all these areas of concern. WHDH was an award winning station and a statistical analysis of media facilities in Boston, as well as in all the cities in the United States, revealed a plethora of voices and a highly diversified ownership of mass media. But the FCC did not have these data at its disposal when it made its decision. Clearly, much of public policy is motivated by serious misconceptions as to the basic nature of mass communications in the United States.

When Senator Pastore (Dem., R.I.) in the Senate and about 100 Congressmen in the House introduced a bill to reverse this decision, the FCC backed down. But the FCC's second thoughts were challenged in the U.S. Court of Appeals in the D.C. Circuit by the Citizens Communication Center and by Black Efforts for Soul in Television. On June 11, 1971, the Court set aside the FCC's revised policy statement. The Court of Appeals held that there must be comparative hearings whenever a licensee is challenged by another applicant at renewal time, that the Commission should consider superior programming service in renewal applications, *and that the Commission should define both quantitatively and qualitatively what constitutes superior programming.*[8]

With broadcast licenses subject to renewal every three years, essentially at the discretion of the FCC and its staff, no broadcaster can now be completely independent of government influence in his programming, news reporting or editorial expression. If the Commission, or just several Commissioners, are displeased with a broadcaster because of his programming, news reporting, or editorial expressions, they need not overtly censor. They can simply find legally acceptable reasons for not renewing his license.

With license renewal possibly depending on the vote of a single Commissioner, the views, prejudices, and whims of each Commissioner (as well as of Senators and Congressmen who are influential with the FCC and, of course, the White House, which appoints the Commissioners) all become a matter for assiduous research, study, and cultivation by every licensee. The desire to "improve" the quality of broadcasting thus shifts the industry's attention away from the audience, whose numbers have always been its primary concern, to the need to placate a small group of men.

Attacking the Jugular

Even the *financial* independence of the broadcast media is now under attack. Thus, the courts have held that broadcasters may not refuse to accept and broadcast "commercials" that attack or criticize advertised products. In this way, the fairness doctrine has been expanded to include countercommercials or *anti*-commercials.

But commercials are the sole source of broadcasting income; no sensible advertiser will purchase advertising on a medium that is required to present attacks upon his advertising claims. And there are no advertising claims that go unchallenged by someone. Advertising for things as innocuous as breakfast foods and hair spray have been attacked, and demands have already been made upon broadcasters for the right to respond. Even public service (free) commercials for such organizations as the United Givers Fund have been considered controversial (blacks feel that whites get too much of the money).

The administrator of this court ruling moreover is the Federal Communications Commission, which thus has the power to determine the broadcaster's economic survival. If today the Commission is still reluctant to force broadcasters to carry counter-commercials, this attitude can change with a change in the Commission's membership. In any case, the power and the threat to use it are now there and constitute an important breach of the media's independence.

Clearly, a major conflict is building for control of the nation's mass communications system. The contending parties are the government and the private sector. The private sector, however, is out of favor with the academicians and intellectuals who help to create an environment of ideas and thereby provide the rationale for public policy.

How did we arrive at this state of affairs? As we have already noted, and as we shall see in the ensuing discussion, a major problem facing the mass media today is, paradoxically, the appalling lack of factual information available about the industry, a situation that necessarily gives rise to myths. In the following chapters we take a closer look at this mythology.

II

The System

Is Television Replacing the Other Media?

One of the reasons for the general impression that television, in particular, has awesome powers is the disappearance of many of the giants in the newspaper field during television's development as the nationwide medium. A year hardly goes by when a big city daily doesn't give up the ghost.

In 1963, the nation's second largest newspaper, the *New York Daily Mirror,* went under. This was followed by the agonizing death of the venerable *New York Herald Tribune* in 1966, and some months later by the demise of the *New York World-Telegram and Sun* and the *New York Journal American*, all of which had a long and respected history in American journalism. Nor is this problem confined to New York City. More recently, as already noted, the *Boston Herald Traveler* folded, as did the *Newark News* in New Jersey and the *Daily News* in Washington, D.C. Indeed nationwide, in the years 1950-1967 when television had its most rapid growth, 330 newspapers, or about 1 out of 5, suspended operation.[1] Today only 43 cities in the United States are left with competing major dailies.

It is easy to generalize from these observations that the newspaper industry is in trouble. Since these difficulties coincided with the growth of television it is also tempting to conclude that newspapers are being replaced by the newer technology. Indeed it is often said that newspapers are becoming an obsolete form of mass communication. The weight of the evidence, however, clearly shows that such conclusions are unfounded.

Available data indicate that newspaper readership in general, has increased. Thus, although the number of dailies has declined from about 2,000 in 1920 to 1,800 in 1973, their circulation has increased from 28 million per day in 1920 to about 63 million per day in 1973. In effect, in a period when the national population more than doubled, and radio and television were introduced, newspaper circulation increased by about 125 percent. Newspaper revenues from advertising increased even more rapidly than circulation during the 1920-1973 period, rising from about $300 million in 1920 to nearly $8 *billion* in 1973.

TABLE 1

Where Advertising Money Goes by Type of
Mass Media—1973
(In Billions of Dollars)

Daily Newspapers	$ 7.7
Television	4.5*
Radio	1.6
Magazines	1.5
Total	$15.3

*Estimated. Includes local advertising.

Source: *Advertising Age,* August 27, 1973. Prepared by McCann-Erickson, Inc., and FCC Releases 06034, 92704

When compared with television, in absolute terms, the importance of the printed medium looms even larger. Thus, the economic fuel that operates America's mass communications system is the advertising expenditures of American business. Over $25 billion was spent on all forms of advertising in the United States in 1973. Of this sum, what is conventionally referred to as the mass media—newspapers, television, radio and magazines—received about $15 billion or over 60 percent, and of these $15 billion, the daily newspaper is the recipient of nearly $8 billion or more than half of the advertising money spent on all the mass media. In addition, newspapers receive over $2 billion a year from subscriptions and sales at newsstands. The newspaper industry's total revenue (exclusive of the wire services) thus approaches $10 billion a year. This is more than twice the revenue received by the entire television broadcasting industry in 1973.

These facts may come as a surprise to the many people who have the mistaken impression that television is today the dominant medium in the United States. Television does command a lot of attention, but in many respects, particularly in economic terms, it is considerably behind newspapers and the printed media.

How then do we explain the high rate of failure among newspapers?

Looking back at the 1950-1967 period we see that while 330 newspapers failed, 303 new dailies were started, an average of 17 new dailies a year. Of the 303 new ventures, 166 survived to become established enterprises. This is a success rate of 55 percent. Significantly, and in this lies the explanation, most of the successes were in cities with a population of under 500,000. The problem of survival is a problem facing newspapers in the big cities.

Why Newspapers Fail

What is troubling the big city newspaper? Excess printing capacity, rising labor costs (specifically, of typesetters), and the inability to adopt radically new technology are some of the problems. But these are not the critical factors. There is a more fundamental problem.

Since advertisers necessarily watch the circulation figures, the two, circulation and advertising, are closely related. Newspaper economists agree that if a big city newspaper's circulation exceeds that of its principal competitor by a 2:1 margin, this will prove fatal to the relatively smaller newspaper no matter how large it might be.

The extreme sensitivity of newspapers to declining circulation is due in large part to the structure of their advertising rates. These are based on a sliding scale whereby substantial advertisers obtain substantial discounts. Thus, a big advertiser can get as much as a 35 percent discount by doubling the amount of space he buys in a single newspaper in a given year. To obtain this discount, the advertiser is encouraged to give all his business to a single newspaper in a given community. That newspaper is frequently the one that has the edge in circulation. So he is induced to take his advertising away from the relatively smaller newspaper and place it in the competing daily. It is the pursuit of the discount that whiplashes the runner-up even though it has a large circulation and tries to compete by lowering its own rates.

The *New York Daily Mirror*, which folded in 1963 when it was the second largest morning newspaper in the United States, had a daily circulation of over 800,000 when it closed down. Nevertheless, it was substantially behind the competing morning tabloid, the *New York Daily News*, and so was the loser in the ensuing advertising war.

The *New York Herald Tribune* faced a similar problem. The *Tribune* died because in the years between 1955 and 1965, its advertising lineage had dropped below the break-even point, or by a total of 1,911,395 lines. This represented $2,675,000 a year in lost revenues, or $390,000 more than the annual wage bill for its 277 printers. The *Tribune* could not have survived even if its printers had decided to work for nothing. Thus even the use of the latest technology, which would have reduced its wage bill, would not have sufficed.[3]

What lies behind the sudden, desperate pressure for newspaper circulation in the nation's big cities?

The explanation is found in the increasing decentralization of America's urban centers. As the wealthy and middle class whites move into the suburbs the retail shopping center and department store branches follow them. And so does the newspaper circulation and advertising revenue that supported the old, well established big city dailies. In effect, social forces outside the industry are reshaping its character in the second half of the twentieth century. The issue is thus not technological but sociological. Newspapers are not becoming technologically obsolete. Rather, their markets are changing location and they are now in a state of transition. The impact of these changes is greatest in the major cities.

Tripping Over the Wire Services

One of the impediments to establishing a new newspaper in a large city is the high cost of subscribing to the major wire services. Wire services are to the newspapers what television networks are to television broadcasting stations—they are their main source of information. (Television network news departments also employ the wire services to supplement their own sources.) Privately owned, these wire services serve as the primary source of nearly all of the national and international news available to the American public.

Implicitly, when we speak of the wire services we refer to the two prominent ones; United Press International (UPI), and the Associated Press (AP). *Editor & Publisher Yearbook*, however lists 312 domestic and foreign features syndicates, ranging from UPI and AP to small one-man operations that use the mails rather than a private wire. It was one such small outfit—The Dispatch News Service (employing the mails), that broke the My Lai massacre story in 1970.

With considerable overlapping, the syndicates that provide straight news and pictures number 212. The editorial features category includes 35 syndicates; the editorial cartoons category, 33; household features, 44; and religious features, 49.

Some of these organizations tend to specialize by serving the media of specific subgroups. Thus the Jewish Telegraphic Agency specializes in news and features of interest to Jewish audiences while the National Catholic News Service focuses on news of interest to Catholics. Other specialized syndicates include the Women's News Service, the Science News Service, Chinese Information Service, and the Auto News Syndicate. But as already noted, it is the services of UPI and AP that are essential for the kind of worldwide, in-depth news coverage needed to be an effective competitor, particularly in the big cities of the United States.

Though both UPI and AP are private organizations with a global communications system, they differ radically in structure. UPI (the smaller of the two) is a private, profit-oriented operation owned entirely by the E. W. Scripps organization since 1907. E. W. Scripps also owns the United Features Syndicate and newspapers in 18 cities and television stations in five cities. The annual cost of operating UPI is approaching $60,000,000.

The AP, on the other hand, is owned by a nonprofit association of newspapers. Founded in 1848, it is today the largest news-gathering organization in the world. Its annual budget exceeds $70,000,000, and its member newspapers together spend many times this figure collecting local and regional news, which is then supplied to the AP.

Nearly all the dailies in America and over half of all the radio and television broadcasting stations subscribe to both the UPI and AP news services. UPI and AP also serve thousands of media abroad. In less than a minute they can transmit a news bulletin to over 104 countries.

Each of the two major wire services employs approximately 2,000 full-time professionals. Nearly one-third of these professionals are journalists posted abroad. In addition, there are thousands of "stringers" who provide information on a call basis, or at irregular intervals.

Since 1951, UPI has offered a service that not only sends news dispatches by wire but, when linked to a typesetting machine, automatically sets them in type in the client's own newspaper office. In 1958, UPI also established an audio network that transmits news for direct broadcast by more than 400 radio stations in the United States.

An important factor limiting the entry of new dailies in the major cities is the relatively high fee required by the major wire services. The two wire services require evidence of survivability in the form of substantial working capital. In addition, a subscriber has to put down a one-year advance and sign a five-year contract. The price of the service, however, is based *not* on subscriber circulation, which for a newcomer would be low, but on the size of the market in which he operates. In the large cities, this involves a very substantial annual cost for just one wire service. When combined with a one-year advance, this means that there is a very stiff entry fee, and double this sum for two major wire

services. This cost could be a serious obstacle for a newcomer, certainly more serious than the presence of television
which, as we shall see later, is not a serious competitor for
newspaper advertising revenue or its audience.

On the Down Staircase: The Radio Networks

The reputation of television as the "spoiler," representing a
powerful competitive force on the media scene is more
deserved for its effect on the radio networks than for any
imagined effect on newspapers. Its impact on the radio
networks can be described in one word—devastating.

For the generation or two that grew up on *Captain
Midnight, The Shadow, Fred Allen, Fiber McGee & Molly,
The Great Gildersleeve,* and *Gabriel Heater*, and who are now
the nation's decision makers, its Congressmen, academicians,
regulators and writers, television left them only fond
memories of the highly successful radio network news and
entertainment medium. It is with some cause, therefore, that
today's opinion makers and policy makers are in awe of the
power of television and inferentially of all mass media. This
experience makes them believe much of the mythology
surrounding mass communications, especially television.

In 1950, before television's explosive growth, the 4
national radio networks were all doing well. ABC, CBS, NBC,
and MBS (Mutual Broadcasting System) together had a
nationwide audience and earned profits of $19 million,
before taxes, on revenues of $106 million. That same year
the four struggling television networks (Dumont, now
defunct, was the fourth) lost $10 million on revenues of $55
million.[4]

Since then, television has drastically changed the radio

business forcing it to become strictly a local medium. The radio network entertainment shows are all gone, replaced by television. Network radio (consisting principally of music and news) has shrunk from gross revenues of $106 million in its heyday to $53 million in 1972, a decline of 50 percent.

In 1972 the four national radio networks together incurred a loss of nearly $2 million, and have been losing several million dollars a year for some time. This has given rise to the widespread belief that radio is in a state of depression, if not on its way out as a mass medium.

The decline of the radio networks, however, should not be confused with the state of well-being of radio broadcasting. By shifting the focus of its attention from a nationwide audience to the local audience, radio broadcasting underwent an unprecedented boom at the very time that radio networking was slipping into oblivion.

In 1950, when television was still in its infancy, there were 2,100 radio stations in the United States. Twenty-three years later, in 1973, there were 5,100 radio stations on-the-air, much more than double the number before television. The revenues of radio broadcasting stations more than tripled in this period, from $334 million in 1950 to $1.5 billion in 1973. The profits more than doubled from $49 million in 1950, to about $120 million in 1973.[5] Radio networks had declined in importance as a source of programming but radio itself prospered as a mass medium.

A number of factors shaped this transformation. These include the explosive growth of the radio audience as a result of low cost transistor radios. The number of radios in the United States increased from 85 million in 1950 to 369 million in 1973. As a result of the rise of suburban commuting, automobile radios alone increased from 18 million sets in use in 1950, to 93 million in 1973.[6] On the other side of the coin, the low cost of entry into radio broadcasting attracted local investors who saw radio as a prestigious small business. Thus, while individual communications companies, particularly the giants, were undergoing internal upheavals, radio broadcasting was expanding.

Creative Destruction

The giants among newspapers, magazines and radio experienced in the 1960's what is referred to by economists as the process of "creative destruction." Suburbanization and the advent of television shook the established corporations to their foundations. Firms that seemed to be the eternal powers with a dominant, deeply entrenched position in mass communications at one moment, were transformed in the next moment into small businesses (for example, the radio networks)—if they survived at all. As a form of mass communication, however, newspapers, magazines, and radio were not rendered obsolete, they boomed. Their internal structures were altered and their giants were humbled but, as industries, they thrived. In a creative, free and open economic environment, power is transitory, almost fleeting, indeed perhaps nonexistent. Who would believe, for example, that *Life* magazine would ever cease publication? The process of creative destruction had removed from the scene a publication that only three short years before had sufficient influence to bring about the resignation of a Supreme Court justice. Like the radio and the newspaper, the magazine was also in the process of change.

The 9,600 weekly, monthly and quarterly magazines and journals published in the United States range in character from the most widely read (*Reader's Digest*: 17 million circulation) to thousands of small and obscure publications that cater to specific needs of different groups of readers. The evidence indicates, however, that the future of the magazine business belongs to the small specialized publications.

To survive today a magazine has to satisfy a special interest. Zoology, occultism, antiques, high fidelity, dressmaking, dogs, bowling, poetry, travel, indeed in almost any subject one inevitably has several publications from which to choose. Similarly, each religious, social, trade, professional and technical group is served by a number of periodicals fighting for a greater share of that market.

The financial support for these publications is based on their specialized readership and the advertiser's interest in reaching just those particular readers. The audience of these publications is defined by the publication's subject matter. Thus, magazines have become the vehicle for advertising special products for special audiences. Advertisers of widely consumed products, on the other hand, look to television to reach the mass audience. The victim of these developments has been the mass circulation magazine which has all but disappeared. Thus, such former giants of the communications industry as *Colliers, Saturday Evening Post, Look,* and *Life* have passed into publishing history.

Initially, the mass circulation magazines tried to compete with television. In the early 1960s *Life* and *Look* fought a circulation battle to see which (like television) could reach the greatest number of subscribers. Indeed *Life* even bought 1.5 million subscribers from the defunct *Saturday Evening Post* in order to reach what proved to be its peak circulation of 8.5 million in 1968. But this larger circulation required higher advertising rates. In 1968, *Life* had to charge $64,000 for a color page, much more than the cost of a minute of prime time on television.

Madison Avenue wouldn't buy. There was a 13 percent

decline in advertising pages that year and the price had to be cut to $54,000 a color page. But the cost of reaching a thousand homes was still too high, about $7.71 compared to $3.60 for television. An important distinction between magazines and television that explains some of this price disparity is the concept of *circulation*. Circulation is the number of buyers or subscribers of the publication. The *readership*, particularly of the general magazine is at least five times that number. In addition, the magazine or any printed medium, can be used for recall by the subscriber. Television, on the other hand, reaches its audience but once with each message. The advantage of television, on the other hand, is that it employs both sight and sound. It also reaches the disinterested viewer who does not flip channels as he would a page in a magazine in order to avoid a message that doesn't interest him. The latter makes readership an unreliable index of an ad's audience. In other words, the television audience is more of a captive than is the self-programmed reader of periodicals.

In the final analysis, advertisers preferred television to magazines as the vehicle for mass marketing. Their decision was also based, in part, on an awareness that the circulation of the major magazines was being subsidized. It didn't reflect a real demand on the part of the public. This is evident from a comparison between the price the public is willing to pay for more specialized magazines and what it is prepared to pay for general (mass) magazines.

Between 1947 and 1970 *Life*'s *newsstand* sales fell from 2.5 million to 210,000 even though it had a relatively low newsstand price of 50 cents. *Look* also sold on the newsstands for only 50 cents. Relatively more specialized magazines such as *Playboy* ($1 a copy) and *Cosmopolitan* ($1 a copy), on the other hand, were able to obtain 80 percent and 88 percent of their circulation, respectively, from newsstand sales despite higher prices. The truly mass circulation magazines with their generalized content could only maintain their huge circulations by practically giving away their publication to subscribers for about 12 cents a copy although it cost the publisher over 40 cents to produce and distribute. The public, it appears, found the content of such magazines of insufficient continuing interest to warrant paying a higher price. This attitude was not lost on the advertisers.[7]

Stopgap measures had been employed in the fight for survival. Several magazines cut their physical size. A mere three-sixteenths-of-an-inch trim in page size reportedly saved *Life* $500,000 a year although most reductions in page size have been substantially greater (*McCall's*, *Ladies Home Journal*, *Esquire*, *Fortune*). But for *Life* magazine such savings merely postponed the inevitable. The only long-term solution for periodicals is to stake out a subgroup in the mass audience that will permit a sharp cutback in costly circulation with a less than proportionate reduction in advertising rates.

This was the path taken by Time, Inc. following the collapse of *Life* magazine. They first marketed *Money*, a consumer's magazine aimed at the middle income shopper. This was followed, about a year later (1974), with *People*, a biography-gossip-news magazine. To avoid the pitfalls introduced by sharply rising postal rates, *People* is not sold by subscription but over-the-counter in supermarkets and drug stores. The new publication has a fulltime staff of only 34. Its price is only 35¢ and its first press run was a relatively modest 1.4 million copies—compared with *Life*'s peak printing of 8.5 million. These more modest proportions have permitted Time, Inc. to lower its advertising rate to one half that required by *Life* in its heyday.

If Time, Inc. can market three or four specialty magazines with circulations of about 2 million each and maintain their present lean operating budgets, they might establish themselves once again as one of the nation's premier magazine publishers. This opportunity is open to anyone, since there is free entry in this field.

To Specialize or Not to Specialize

The demise of *Look* and *Life* has frightened other mass circulation magazines. These include magazines that specialize in very large subgroups, such as men or women. One such publication sought unsuccessfully to anticipate and to fend off the fate of the more general mass circulation magazines.

In an analysis of magazine economics that appeared in the *Columbia Journalism Review*, Chris Welles compared the attempts of *McCall's* and the *Ladies Home Journal* to face up to these problems.[8] He noted that the major magazines catering to the women's market have a dual personality. They are mass circulation publications that serve a special audience. Thus *McCall's*, which had a 1970 circulation of over 8 million and *Ladies Home Journal*, which had a circulation of nearly 7 million specialize in the homemaker market. By comparison men's magazines tend to serve smaller audiences. Thus *Playboy*, the largest "man's" magazine, has half the circulation reported by the largest "woman's" magazine. Women's interests are much more homogeneous which contributes to the large size of their audience.

Despite the mass circulation character of the leading women's magazines they have substantial advertiser support because they are aimed at the homemaker who buys most of the food, drugs, toiletries, and related goods that are subject to mass marketing. Nevertheless, fearing the fate of the general mass circulation magazines, *McCall's*, despite a reputedly profitable operation, made a major attempt to break away from the homemaker format. In 1969, it brought in Shana Alexander, a *Life* columnist, to serve as editor in a premature attempt to reach a sophisticated "concerned" subgroup of the mass women's markets. She shifted the focus of *McCall's* away from the home to world issues. The result: advertisers, fearing a loss of the homemaker atmosphere which the old format had provided for their products, began to withdraw their support, while the *Ladies Home Journal*, which retained its homemaker format, saw its revenues increase by 19 percent in 1969-1970.

McCall's eventually brought in a new editor who tried, unsuccessfully, to recapture the old *McCall's* clientele. In 1973, its owner, the Norton Simon Corporation, sold *McCall's* to a more optimistic investor, the owners of the Hyatt Hotels. The *McCall's* experiment, although unsuccessful, was farsighted.

The cost of maintaining mass circulation magazines is rapidly becoming prohibitive. As Welles pointed out in his article, the cost of paper will double between 1970 and 1975, printing costs will probably increase 50 percent, and the postal rates will go up 142 percent. But major increases in advertising rates are almost out of the question since mass circulation magazines are already more expensive than television, the principal vehicle for access to large audiences. Thus, the only alternative is to increase subscription rates. This, however, will cut down on the circulation of supposedly mass circulation magazines.

It is not easy to back down; the transition is costly. Significantly, the audience that *McCall's* tried to reach was eventually tackled with some success, but on a much smaller scale, by an entirely new publication, *Ms.*, which focuses on the feminist market.

The process of creative destruction observed at work in network radio is thus also at work in the magazine field.

Such reputedly powerful organizations as Time, Inc., Curtis Publishing Co., and Crowell Collier, simply could not influence the public or the advertisers to continue to support their publications. This is a strange situation for enterprises supposedly in the business of influencing their customers. It stands in stark contrast to the mythology that attributes to these "media baronies" the awesome ability to seize their audiences by their collective psyches and to shape their attitudes on almost anything of importance.

On the Fringe

Several substantial, though relatively minor, media operate on the fringe of mass communications. They are not significant in terms of advertising but are very important in noncommercial matters. One such medium is the weekly newspaper. These publications serve a specifically defined geographic area with neighborhood news. The local merchants, artisans, and families use its columns and classified sections to communicate with one another.

In 1973 there were 8,800 weeklies published in the United States with a combined circulation exceeding 28 million. Their circulation increased over 45 percent in 15 years. The weeklies claim a readership of 111 million or about 4 readers per copy.

A central advertising agency—The American Newspaper Representatives Incorporated—serves most of the weeklies as a clearing house for national advertising. The suburban market which many weeklies serve has grown substantially in wealth as well as in size in recent years. These developments have not gone unnoticed by the major communications companies. Thus, Time, Inc. purchased over 25 weekly newspapers in the Chicago area in 1969.

There are also media that cater to large special groups. Most of these fall into one of three categories: black, religious, or foreign language. There are currently 163 black-oriented publications in the United States with a total circulation of 5.1 million or nearly one copy for each black family in America. Almost 40 percent of this circulation is accounted for by just three publications: *Ebony* (monthly: 1,222,000); *Jet* (weekly: 565,000); and *Muhammad Speaks* (weekly: 530,000). In addition, there are about 385 radio stations with some black programming, including 67 devoted entirely to black programming. At least one such station is located in every major city in the United States, and in many smaller southern cities.[9]

There has been a substantial change in the character of the black press since 1945, a change that reflects the evolution of black self-consciousness. In 1945 the three "giants" in this field were: the Pittsburgh *Courier*, the Chicago *Defender* and the Baltimore *Afro-American.* Today the *Defender*'s circulation has dropped to 33,300 from 202,000 in 1945 and the *Courier*'s circulation has dropped from 257,000 to 48,800. Only the *Afro-American* has maintained its 1945 circulation, in spite of the fact that the black population has increased by about 50 percent during this period.

Two of the replacements for these conservative publications are *Muhammad Speaks* (530,000) and the *Black Panther* (110,000). *Muhammad Speaks* is published for the Black Muslim sect by a professional staff of 32 journalists and editors, only half of them Muslims. The acting editor in Chicago is a Harvard graduate; the New York editor is a graduate of the Columbia University School of Journalism. Although it is the largest black newspaper in the United

States, *Muhammad Speaks* does not depend on advertising for revenue.[10] Aside from private contributions it was reported to have received a $3 million loan from Libya in 1971.

The *Black Panther*, on the other hand, is a tabloid produced and distributed by volunteers. It competes with a number of other smaller but similar tabloids that employ the production and distribution techniques of the radical underground press, discussed in another chapter.

The foreign language media also operate on the fringe of the major media. Once an extremely important source of information and entertainment for millions of foreign-born Americans, their popularity has declined with the decline in immigration. Nevertheless there are still 341 general interest periodicals published in 26 different languages, with a combined circulation exceeding 2 million. The largest circulation is credited to 29 Spanish language newspapers which have a combined circulation of about 450,000. They serve the only foreign language audience in the United States that is still growing. In addition, 743 radio stations in the United States broadcast some foreign language programs.

But the largest group of mass media focusing on a special audience in the United States are the 1,300 religiously-oriented newspapers and periodicals. While many of them have very small circulations, 19 major religious periodicals, each with circulations exceeding 400,000 have a combined circulation of more than 30 million, or nearly one copy for every two households in the United States.[11] One such publisher, the Worldwide Church of God, which has only 85,000 churchgoers, mails out free over 3 million copies of *Plain Truth* each month. In 1973, the sect received over $50 million from members and sympathizers.[12]

In general, religious publications are financed through dues and donations paid to the main religious organizations, commercial advertising plays a relatively unimportant role in their support.

The media based on geographical identity (weeklies), race, religion, and ethnic backgrounds offer the mass media serious competition in the realm of ideas. Their impact is small in economic terms but, contrary to the accepted mythology, they are important opinion makers.

The Age of Television

Without eliminating any of the existing forms of mass communication, television has established itself as the sole *national* medium. At the fulcrum of today's television system in the United States are the three networks with which three out of every four television stations are affiliated. The local broadcast stations provide the networks with regular, assured access to their local television audiences. In exchange, the networks provide these stations with programs through much of the day. Not only are these programs provided free, but the stations are paid a percentage of the advertising revenue that the networks receive from national advertisers.

Stations that by virtue of their geographical location reach large audiences cost the advertisers a higher price for their inclusion in the network lineup than stations located in smaller markets. Each network affiliate receives a portion of its price. Overall, network affiliates receive about 12 percent of the advertising money received by the networks (and free programming). These funds account for approximately 11 percent of the total revenue received by television broadcasting stations.[13] The rest of the broadcasters' income is obtained from local advertisers and from the national "spot" market, discussed below.

The size of the audience "delivered" to the advertiser by the network is a function of the number of cities in the network lineup, the time of day the commercial is shown, and the popularity of the program in which it was included. These three factors determine the price paid by the advertiser.

The broadcasters have practically no say over any of these factors. They cannot effect the number of persons choosing to live in their market area, nor the caliber or popularity of the network's choice of programs. Their facilities are in a very real sense conduits for the national television networks. Programming decisions are made by local broadcasters principally for the early morning and late evening hours and for the weekends. These generally account for about half of their broadcasting hours. But the networks supply the programs for the prime hours when the audiences are largest.

For those hours for which the networks do not provide programs the broadcasters buy programs from independent producers and from the "syndication market," which offers a large number of programs that have already been seen on television (reruns). The revenue obtained by broadcasters during those hours when they program for themselves, is derived from local advertisers (used car dealers, department stores, etc.) and the "spot market," consisting of regional and national advertisers who wish to advertise in selected markets rather than across-the-board in a network lineup. This "spot" money is channeled to broadcasters (by the advertising agencies) through station representatives who are, in effect, time brokers for the local stations. Most of these brokers or representatives are located in New York City. Some sixty such brokers represent nearly all the television and radio stations in the United States.

Local advertisers account for about 39 percent of the average broadcaster's revenue and the regional and national "spot" market accounts for about 50 percent of his revenue. The balance (11 percent), as already noted, is received from the networks.[14]

Looking at the television industry as a whole, including the three television networks, we find a different composition for advertising revenue due to the substantial sum retained by the networks, as shown in Table 2.

TABLE 2

Sources of Television Revenue—1972

SOURCE	REVENUE	% OF TOTAL
Network	$1,687,000,000	46%
Spot	1,167,000,000	32
Local	778,000,000	22
Total	$3,632,000,000	100%

*Including the three networks.

Source: FCC Release 05963 (August 1973), Table 1.

Network Profitability

How rich are the television networks (—not including their broadcasting stations)? When *combined* the three networks would rank 113th in sales among *Fortune* magazine's list of the 500 largest industrial corporations. (Taken separately, of course, each network would rank still lower.) Not only are 113 industrial companies larger than the three television networks *combined*, but so are 22 retailers and six transportation companies.[15]

In 1972 the combined profit derived from the programming activities of the three television networks totaled $111 million on sales (after commissions) of $1,271 million. That comes to an 8.7 percent return on revenues, before taxes. This return on sales is equal to the average for American industry as a whole. Significantly, the five television broadcasting stations which each network owns yielded, as a group, nearly the same dollar amount of profits as did the three networks.

The five television broadcasting stations owned by each network are among the most profitable in the United States. In 1972 these 15 broadcasting stations, as a group, grossed $327 million, or approximately one-fifth the combined gross revenue of the other 648 commercial television stations for which FCC data were available. The profits (before taxes) of those 15 network owned television stations totaled $102 million in 1972. By comparison all of the other 648 television stations together earned profits of $339 million, before taxes, that year, or only slightly more than three times the profits earned by the 15 network owned stations.[16] The networks' stations are clearly money making machines. As a result of their extraordinary profitability, these stations have given the television industry as a whole an undeserved reputation for enormous profits. The entire industry—networks and all broadcasting stations combined—is not as profitable as dozens of industrial corporations, a matter discussed in more detail in Chapter IX.

Because of their financial importance to the networks, the 15 network owned television stations are, from the regulatory standpoint, the Achilles heel of the television industry. While network program operations are beyond the *direct* reach of government regulation, all broadcasting stations are licensed and regulated by the government. As we see in the next chapter, they are, as a result, the one lever of the mass communications system in the United States upon which the government has a firm grip.

Media Ownership

How Many Can Play

In the United States, unlike any other country in the world, the publication of newspapers, magazines and books involves virtually no regulation or licensing, something that is not true even for the local drug store, building contractor, or restaurant. The commercial broadcasting stations, on the other hand, though entirely privately owned, are licensed by the federal government. The principal mechanism by which the government seeks to exercise some authority over radio and television broadcasting is through the issuance and threatened withdrawal of these broadcasting licenses.

While all of the worthwhile broadcast licenses have long since been assigned, looking back we can agree with the many critics who point out that the degree of differentiation among competing applicants was generally illusory and that the assignment of a broadcaster's license was more often than not a reward for the group or company represented by the more clever or better connected attorney.

Many of these critics would have preferred to see these

licenses auctioned off to the highest bidder instead of being awarded free to the winning applicant. But delivering these licenses into the hands of the wealthiest contestants would hardly have been an improvement over the admittedly deficient system that was used.

In fact, some form of auction was involved. After exhaustive and expensive comparative hearings, nearly half of those who originally received a permit from the FCC to build a television station (preliminary to licensing) eventually sold their permit to the highest bidder. The profits, however, benefited the seller, not the public purse. A better approach would have been to conduct a lottery among the qualified contenders. The result would have been a considerable savings in legal fees and government expense. The winner of the lottery might then have been required to pay a fee representing the license's economic potential so that the public purse would have capitalized on some of the license's value, instead of allowing the first licensee all of the benefit from the capital gain. But that, of course, is all a part of history.

Whatever the original flaws in the government's method of assigning broadcast licenses, most of the really valuable licenses have long since gravitated into the hands of large broadcast companies referred to as "group owners."

By law, however, no group owner can own more than seven television stations, nor more than one in the same market (city). For reasons we shall take up in some detail in Chapter V, the government designed the televison communications system so that it consists of hundreds of broadcasting stations each covering a relatively small geographic area, rather than regional coverage with each region being served by several stations.

In part, the highly fractionalized ownership of America's broadcast communications reflects a deeply rooted national distrust of powerful social, political and economic institutions. Under America's unique banking system for example, there are over 13,000 banks as contrasted to fewer than eight in most other countries. And none of the nation's 13,000 banks may have an office outside of its home state, a rule intended to prevent the development of a nationwide money monopoly. Even the powers of the central banks, the Federal Reserve System and the Federal Home Loan Bank, are divided among a dozen or more regional and district banks. Similarly, America's educational system is based on tens of thousands of local school districts, and here the state governments have only limited authority and the federal government has virtually no authority at all. Small wonder that ownership should be such an important concern in the operation of America's mass communications. But as we shall see later, the application of this policy to television was a major error.

The communications system, however, is further divided between the owners of the facilities (newspapers, radio and television broadcasting stations) and the producers of the content transmitted by these facilities. The producers of most of the content are the two major wire services and the three television networks. This distinction between the ownership of the distribution facilities and the production of the content is not clear-cut; newspapers and radio and television stations also produce some of their own material, while some wire services own important newspapers, and the networks own lucrative radio and television broadcasting stations. Still, the distinction is important in identifying the centers of decision-making within the industry.

The owners of communications facilities—newspapers and broadcasting stations—theoretically have the power (and responsibility) to decide what their local audience will see, hear, and read. In practical terms, however, television broadcasters have almost no say in the content of network programs or in their selection. And for most station owners, production costs are too high to permit them to produce effective programming on their own. In addition, the flow of news into newspapers and radio stations today is so voluminous that there is barely time to read through what is available for use each day, much less to check its veracity. For all practical purposes, the owners of the mass media are as dependent on their program and information suppliers for the content they transmit to the public as a retail merchant is dependent on his wholesaler for the merchandise he sells.

Thus, despite the atomized ownership structure of the communications facilities, most of the news and entertainment received by the American public are produced by five corporations: UPI, AP, CBS, ABC, and NBC. *Yet none of these enterprises are licensed or regulated in their production activities by any government agency—federal, state, or local.*

Only by threatening the networks' ownership of their lucrative broadcasting stations, which *are* licensed, or by regulations affecting the broadcasters' relationship with the networks, can the regulatory authority (FCC) influence the program decisions of the radio and television networks. Since newspapers are not licensed by any authority, the wire services are protected even from this indirect control.

As a result of the FCC's arm's-length relationship with the networks, there is an intense preoccupation with broadcasting stations. By changing the rules governing broadcasting, the FCC hopes to effect changes in programming. There are several methods by which this result is obtained.

Rules of the Game

Once the FCC has granted a license to operate a broadcasting station, it retains the authority to review the assignment every three years. At that time, the license can be renewed (which most are), or revoked (which is very rare) or reissued with conditions. (Its sale to others requires FCC approval, generally readily obtained.) At each stage, the FCC examines the station's programming.

Then there are the rules that limit the *use* of the license—the equal time provisions, the fairness doctrine, and the antitrust and libel laws. Despite these rules and the opportunity to review the stations' programming the FCC is plagued by the fear that the industry, more particularly the networks, will not perform in a manner that the government deems to be socially desirable. To ensure such (undefined) behavior, the FCC has enacted regulations that restrict the number of hours of programming that a station may receive from the networks.

This rule, enacted in 1971, sought to force the creation and growth of independent production companies in order to get greater diversity in programming. The results, thus far, have been extremely disappointing. The broadcasters are unable to spend the kind of money that would make the highly risky program production business attractive to newcomers. The consequence is a plethora of game shows which are relatively inexpensive, but far from the uplifting character intended by the promoters of the 1971 anti-network rule. Television station owners, with few exceptions, do not have the economic capacity to produce quality programming on a regularly scheduled basis. Yet for some unexplained reason, the FCC has for years looked upon the licensee as the arbiter of the programming he broadcasts. The commission has built a complex regulatory superstructure on this myth.

The FCC limited the *number* of stations a company could own (regardless of the station's size or location). This, it was hoped, in conjunction with the *duopoly rule* (which prohibits the ownership of more than one radio station and more than one television station, respectively, within the same market), would preclude the domination of a market—or the political dominance of an audience—by a single firm.

This is not an unreasonable concern. Working from the unlikely though possible premise that all media owners are scoundrels, one can at least have confidence that the conflicting interests of different owners will permit the public, should it wish, to obtain information regarding all sides of an issue with relative ease. In this respect, diverse ownership of media is important. However, a highly fractionated system which precludes the presence of large though competing media owners could lead to a different type of problem. Small size can result in timidity. It can deprive the nation of powerful media groups whose voice can be heard on the national scene. The media should have the power to stand up to the government if the public is to be served.

The media need organizations capable of resisting Congressional indictments, affording the legal fees needed to bring issues to the Supreme Court, and making their voice heard on matters of principle. True, rich and influential organizations do not always rise to the occasion but their *ability* to do so provides a necessary bulwark against an overbearing government bureaucracy.

Some of the Results

Interestingly enough, no firm has actually exploited the existing rules to their limit. Thus, no firm currently owns its entire permitted quota of 21 broadcasting media (seven each of TV, AM, and FM). The largest agglomerations of broadcasting facilities (ABC, Inc. and CBS, Inc.) consist of 19 stations.

But the number of stations (or newspapers) owned by a corporation is no indication of the true size of the organization. This can be determined only by the size of the combined audience reached by the several media it owns. The FCC does not keep a record of this information nor does it design its policies on the basis of the size of the audience reached. It relies only on the number of media owned. This can and has resulted in serious errors in policy making.

Exactly how big, in terms of audience reached, *are* the large media organizations? This question was the subject of a massive computerized study directed by the author on behalf of the National Association of Broadcasters and subsequently filed with the FCC.[1] The following discussion draws extensively from the findings of this research.

Thus it was found that at the peak of the broadcast day, the Westinghouse Corporation, which owns 14 broadcast stations (five TV, seven AM, and two FM), has access to 6.8 million homes or 11 percent of the nation. By comparison, the Storer Broadcasting Corporation, which owns and operates 18 stations (six TV, seven AM, five FM), reaches only 3.3 million homes or 5 percent of the nation at the peak of the broadcast day, about half the audience reached by Westinghouse despite Westinghouse's smaller number of broadcasting stations. Similarly, radio station KRLA alone reaches over 1 percent of the nation or 757,000 homes, while the eight radio stations owned by Lester G. Spencer together reach only 65,000 homes. Clearly, a straight facility count does not provide a realistic index of the number of homes reached by the owners of broadcast media.

Significantly, if we rank the nation's media owners by the size of the audience they reach, we find that the three largest companies are based exclusively on broadcasting, which is regulated. The unregulated newspaper organizations, controlled solely by the forces of the market place, appear for the first time in the fourth position (McCormick-Patterson), and next in the seventh position (Newhouse). Apparently the market place is more restrictive than government policy.

Equally significant is the fact that there are no controls over statewide ownership; the FCC limitation on the ownership of broadcast facilities applies nationally and its duopoly rule applies within a market. As a result, in 28 states and the District of Columbia, there are communications companies with access to over 50 percent of the homes in the state.

Apparently, as far as ownership of the broadcasting media is concerned, public policy rests principally on tradition and myth, rather than on any attempt to identify and deal with real social and economic problems.

Gatekeepers or Barons

Although the *owners* of communications facilities (newspapers and broadcasting stations) are strategically placed in the flow of information and entertainment, they rarely exercise this power on a day-to-day basis. Rather, they set overall policy and then rely on their staff (and on the major news services and the networks). In this respect, media owners are but one of several gatekeepers past whom the content of the mass media must flow. They exercise their power principally through the selection of station managers and newspaper editors who in turn, select the first line of gatekeepers, the producers, directors, reporters and writers.

Yet group owners, those who own a number of media, have been referred to by their critics as "media barons." Historically, this title carries with it somewhat sinister connotations of the muckraker era when the collusive and antisocial behavior of a number of powerful industrialists shocked the nation into the enactment of the antitrust laws and the creation of the Federal Trade Commission.

But the proper operation of the mass media is even more important than the proper functioning of industrial enterprises. When information is withheld or distorted, it is difficult to galvanize public opinion into acting upon important social, economic, and political problems. Indeed, many of the early muckrakers relied on the press to bring the facts to the public.

Thus it is argued that while as a practical matter, news and entertainment are provided by "wholesalers" (that is, networks and wire services), the broadcaster and his subordinates are still free, if they so wish, to reject network programs, buy elsewhere, and edit the news according to their own point of view. Such critics are concerned that the present ownership structure of the communication system may have concentrated too much *political* power in the hands of the owners of the nation's broadcasting stations.

This is not a simple issue to resolve, for it is not an easy matter to determine to what extent an owner of media, even if he were the only owner of all local media (and such a monopoly exists nowhere in the United States), has the power to dominate the local political environment.

A first step in coming to grips with this issue is to measure the "reach" of a media owner's properties—the size of his actual audience. (We shall leave for the next chapter the even more problematic question of his ability to influence this audience.) This is not an easy task, since among other things it involves different types of media (newspapers, radio, and television) and each medium has its own statistical measures and its own definition of "audience."

The data that have to be assembled thus represent a combination of three different concepts of audience. In each instance, they represent the exposure which an owner can expect his media to receive at a given moment but the concept of the "moment" also varies with the medium. The three concepts are: (1) The sales of a newspaper in an average day, which is less than its readership, since, on the average, more than one person reads each copy of a newspaper; (2) The number of homes tuned-in to a radio station in an average week; and (3) the number of homes watching a television station during a moment in prime time (7:00 P.M.-11:00 P.M.). The use of these different measures is dictated by the type of statistics employed by each medium in its day-to-day operations.

Access to the Nation

As of June, 1970, there were only 13 group owners in the United States who, through their ownership of combinations of press, radio, and television facilities could, at a given moment in time reach 5 percent or more of the nation's population. The largest audience was reached by ABC, Inc. On the average, in prime time, its 19 broadcast properties reached a total audience of approximately 9.5 million homes, or 16 percent of the nation. As a network, however, its *programs* reached a much larger proportion of the population through affiliated stations that are owned by others but who carry the network's programs. In this sense, the CBS and NBC networks reached even more homes than ABC. This, however, relates to the production of the content of programs rather than to the ownership of facilities—a distinction too often overlooked in discussing media ownership and the so-called power of the media.

Table 3 is a list of the largest group owners in the nation—those whose combined media reach 5 percent or more of the nation's homes. The fact that newspapers are not regulated by the government, yet they contribute to the large size of only five of the 13 national giants points to the myth of the greater effectiveness of the government over the marketplace in containing economic power.

TABLE 3

Significant Owners of Mass Media*—1970

OWNER OF FACILITIES	% OF THE NATION'S HOMES REACHED
1. ABC, Inc.	16%
2. Westinghouse	11
3. CBS, Inc.	11
4. McCormick-Patterson[†]	9
5. NBC, Inc. (RCA)	9
6. RKO (General Tire)	8
7. Newhouse[†]	7
8. Cowles-Ridder[†]	6
9. Metromedia	6
10. Capital Cities	6
11. Storer	5
12. Scripps-Howard	5
13. Hearst[†]	5

*Media groups that reach 5 percent or more of the nation's homes.
[†]Groups owning newspapers.

Source: M. H. Seiden & Associates, Inc., *Special Study* (1971), FCC Docket 18110.

Thus at the national level the evidence indicates that, while potential national influence accrues to any organization that commands the attention of over 5 percent of the nation, no group of media owners can effectively reach, much less sway, more than a small minority of the population at any moment in time simply through its ownership of the facilities of mass communication.

From the standpoint of *cumulative reach*, a television station probably reaches nearly every home in its signal's coverage area in the course of a week. If we apply this broader weekly viewing measure, (as we had to in the case of radio listening) ABC, Inc.'s facilities reach an additional 15 percent of the nation's homes; NBC, an additional 16 percent, and CBS, an additional 17 percent. This cumulative viewing is referred to in the communications industry as the *net weekly circulation*. This additional viewing produces the following estimates of the audience of all the facilities *owned* by each network (expressed as a percent of the nation's homes): ABC, 31%; CBS, 28%; NBC, 25%.

No other organization's facilities exceed this weekly reach. But, as already noted, the network distribution system of affiliated stations that brings ABC, CBS, and NBC programs into virtually every community in the nation constitutes a much more significant *reach* than that obtained by the networks through their ownership of broadcasting stations.

Because as producers of programming the three networks reach virtually every home in the nation, the government's concern over the ownership of broadcasting stations is of little value or meaning. In effect, a large part of public regulation is founded upon a myth, the myth that the owners of broadcasting stations determine the content of the programs transmitted to the general public.

At the State Level

At the state level, things become a bit stickier. There are few, if any, statewide magazines or statewide dailies or statewide broadcasting stations; but a media group, properly assembled, can make a group owner's views a statewide affair.

Assume the worst, that a group owner at the state level lines up his media behind a specific candidate or issue. The effect of this coordinated effort will be limited to the extent that there are competing owners of comparable audience reach in the same state (assuming that they don't collude). The problem then is not only the size of the largest media owner's audience, but the degree to which there are competing media organizations of equal size.

In Georgia, for example, the Cox Broadcasting Company reaches an estimated 83 percent of the homes in the state and the next largest media organization in that state reaches only 17 percent of the homes. The state of Georgia does not lack media or media owners; there are 286 different media owners in Georgia, but most of them are small, local operations, or are located in surrounding states with broadcast or newspaper circulation to Georgia. As a consequence, there are no large media groups capable of countervailing the Cox organization. Under such circumstances one must simply rely on the basic fairness of the dominant media owner and hope that he will not attempt to dominate. But this is a rather weak straw.

At the other extreme, it is probably equally bad to have a total absence of large media organizations at the state level. A highly localized structure would put a state's mass media at the mercy of public relations men. For without the investigative reporting staff which only large organizations can afford, the small newspapers and broadcasting stations have to rely on government press releases in their statewide coverage. This can be at least as dangerous as a single, dominant group owner.

Table 4 focuses on only those states with very large media groups. Included in the table is the audience reach of the second largest media group in that state. In all, 28 states and the District of Columbia appear on this list. Attention is called to Minnesota, Nevada, and Rhode Island, where the largest group owner reaches every home in the state.

Viewed from a different perspective, it is probably of some national significance to know which media owners have a significant position in more than one state. Reducing our cut-off points to a 25 percent reach, an analysis of the data shows that there are four multi-state group owners each of whom has access to over 25 percent of the homes in five different states. They are: ABC, Cowles-Ridder, Newhouse, and Scripps-Howard. Three corporations each have this position in four states. They are: CBS, NBC (RCA), and Westinghouse. Similarly, four corporations hold a dominant position in three states. They are: Bonneville International (the Mormon Church), Capital Cities Broadcasting, Harriscope Stations, and RKO (General Tire). Beyond this point there are 15 groups and corporations playing a dominant role in each of two different states, and 60 groups or corporations with a more than 25 percent share of the audience each in just one state.

It should be noted that although the data indicate that there is some ground for concern regarding media ownership at the state level there are no rules for media ownership within a state. At the national level, on the other hand, there is a size limitation but it lacks a rationale.

TABLE 4

Dominant Media Owners by State*—1970

STATE	LARGEST GROUP OWNER	PROPORTION OF HOMES REACHED	
		LARGEST OWNER*	NEXT IN SIZE
Arizona	Central Newspapers, Inc.	54%	45%
Connecticut	WTIC	59	20
Delaware	Wilmington Journal	55	43
Dist. of Col.	Post-Newsweek Stns.	96	74
Georgia	Cox Broadcasting Company	83	17
Idaho	Bonneville Int'l. Corp.	57	25
Illinois	Patterson Family	68	40
Iowa	Cowles-Ridder	65	48
Kentucky	WHAS, Inc.	68	23
Maine	Guy Gannett Bcstg.	79	52
Maryland	Hearst Corp.	58	45
Massachusetts	Group W—Westinghouse Bcstg. Co.	62	60
Michigan	Evening News Assn.	54	28
Minnesota	Cowles-Ridder	100	29
Montana	Garryowen Stns.	52	38
Nebraska	Herald Corp.	60	38
Nevada	Southwestern Operating Company	100	26
New Hampshire	Group W—Westinghouse Bcstg. Co.	60	36
North Dakota	WDAY Stns. Forun Publishing Co.	53	47
Oklahoma	WKY T.V. System, Inc.	69	30
Oregon	Newhouse S.I.	89	29
Pennsylvania	Group W—Westinghouse Bcstg. Co.	51	46
Rhode Island	Providence Jrnl. Co.	100	56
South Dakota	Midcontinent Bcstg. Co.	61	40
Tennessee	Scrips-Howard Bcstg. Co.	51	24
Utah	Glassman A.L.	98	68
Virginia	Richmond Newspapers	50	33
Wisconsin	Journal Co.	75	27
Wyoming	Frontier Bcstg. Stns.	53	38

*Those reaching 50% or more of the homes in the state.

Source: M. H. Seiden & Associates, Inc. *Special Study (1971)* FCC Docket 18110.

The Barons in the Market Place

The third and the most controversial level of concern regarding private ownership of the mass media is in the cities. For some inexplicable reason, the cities have been of greater concern to the federal regulatory authorities than the states. The duopoly rule (you can't own more than one property in each type of medium), which applies only to the cities, seems adequate in itself as a control over domination by a single owner. Nevertheless, the FCC persists in playing around with its rules at this level. One of the complicating features of the city or market is the definition of its size.

Among the most common definitions of "market" is the government's Standard Metropolitan Statistical Area (SMSA). This is a grouping of contiguous counties in and around a city which forms a market based on the location of the population. There is, however, a fairly long time lag in the adjustment of the SMSA definition of a market to shifts in the population, but more important, as we shall see, it is not always an accurate reflection of the economics of the market place.

The political jurisdiction of the city is sometimes employed to define the market, but this, too, lacks an economic foundation being based on law and historical precedence.

More recently, the American Research Bureau (ARB), a private audience research firm, developed the concept of ADI (Area of Dominant Influence). This is a communications-oriented concept now in wide use in which every one of the more than 3,000 counties in the United States is assigned to some market based on the location of the television stations that command the majority of the viewing hours reported for that county. Altogether, there are about 204 ADI markets in the continental United States. The ADI concept is the most valid basis for defining integrated geographic and economic units for the purpose of analyzing mass communications since it defines a market from the standpoint of the advertiser.

Commuter mobility, discussed in the last chapter, has led to the development of suburban satellite communities around the urban core and the decentralization of retail sales through widely scattered shopping centers. Consequently, the communications media have become the binding force in today's retail markets, which underlies the birth of the ADI concept. Although based on the television audience, it is a concept now being used in planning newspaper advertising as well.

The importance of the definition for public policy lies in the fact that the larger the size of the market, the greater the number of competing media and competing media owners attributed to the market. Thus the use of the SMSA definition by the FCC led the Commission, in 1969, to adopt a policy that virtually wiped out the multi-million dollar Boston Herald Traveler Corporation.

The Boston SMSA consists of just 4 counties. However, the Boston television signals serve an ADI of 16 counties, including 7 in New Hampshire and one each in Connecticut and Vermont.

By relying on the antiquated SMSA concept the FCC credited Boston with only five television signals. Under the ADI concept, the market originates eight television signals and receives 16 more from adjoining markets. Similarly, the FCC credited Boston with only 19 radio signals based on the SMSA concept, while the ADI concept credits it with originating 68 signals. The Boston ADI is also served by 41 dailies (of which each of 17 have a daily circulation in five figures) and 140 weeklies.

Overall, the Boston ADI has access to 257 media originating in that market, owned by 190 different groups, individuals, or corporations. The FCC data speak of only 27 media—5 television signals, 19 radio signals, and three dailies. It is because of these erroneous data that the FCC felt that the Boston market could use greater diversification of media ownership and, as a result, withdrew the license of WHDH-TV, whose parent company also owned a major Boston newspaper and radio station. As already noted elsewhere in this book, this led to the collapse of the entire enterprise, reducing the number of media available to the Boston public.

The Role of Size

The greater the number of large group owners in the market, the more intense the competition. But a person located in almost any part of a market will be reached by many more media owners than just those able to reach more than a quarter or half of the population. For example, a person living in a market may or may not be reached by one of the major group owners. It all depends on where in the market he lives and works, for there are numerous other media and media owners in the market, though they may cover much smaller sections of the city.

The center of the market is probably the area of greatest overlap of media and media owners. Generally speaking, the farther one travels from the center of the market, the fewer the alternative "voices" available—but also the thinner the population density. In this respect, the number of different media correlates with density of the population. This is understandable: a larger population attracts a larger number of advertisers who, in turn, are able to support a larger number of media.

The largest media owner, in terms of market distribution, is Samuel Newhouse, whose 21 newspapers, 5 television stations and 3 radio stations provide him with a substantial share (over 25 percent) of 11 different markets. Next in line is ABC, Cowles—Ridder, and Westinghouse, all able to reach 25 percent or more of 9 markets. Capital Cities has a major position in 8 markets, and RKO and Scripps-Howard each, in 7 markets. There were four media owners each with major positions in 6 markets, five owners each with major positions in 5 markets, and so forth as summarized in Table 5.

All in all, in 1970 there were 236 media owners with access to 25 percent or more of the homes in each of one or more markets in the United States.

For a well rounded view of what concerns the government (FCC and Justice Department) in matters of media ownership, we must also note their current worry over cross-media

TABLE 5

Multi-Market Dominance—1970

NUMBER OF MARKETS	NUMBER OF OWNERS WITH ACCESS TO 25% [+]HOMES
11	1
10	0
9	3
8	1
7	2
6	4
5	5
4	10
3	14
2	32
1	164
Total Number of Major Owners	236

Source: M. H. Seiden & Associates, Inc. *Special Study* (1971) FCC Docket 18110.

ownership, that is, the ownership of different media by a single owner (or corporation), serving the same market. This is the issue that did in the Boston Herald Traveler Corporation.

This concern on the part of the government is oddly timed. By 1972, as shown in Table 6, cross-media ownership involving radio and newspapers was at its lowest level in over 25 years. This is true both in absolute numbers of radio stations as well as relative to the total number of radio stations. Thus, in 1950, 472 radio stations were owned by newspapers. This was 22.6 percent of the total. By 1972, the number had fallen to 318 stations and only 7.5 percent of the industry.

In the case of television stations, the current situation cannot be compared with 1950, since there were only 97 commercial television stations in the entire country at that time and 690 in 1972. But proportionate to the total, newspaper ownership of television broadcasting has also been declining, and stood at 25.5 percent in 1972.

TABLE 6

*Newspaper Control of Broadcasting
in the United States*

YEAR	TOTAL NO. AM RADIO STATIONS	RADIO: % OWNED BY NEWSPAPERS	TOTAL NO. TELEVISION STATIONS	TELEVISION: % OWNED BY NEWSPAPERS
1945	942	27.7%	9	11.1%
1950	2,086	22.6	97	42.0
1955	2,669	17.4	439	34.0
1960	3,506	12.2	533	32.8
1965	4,039	9.6	598	29.0
1972	4,252	7.5	690	25.5

Source: *Broadcasting Yearbook,* (1972.)

C. Sterling, "Newspaper Ownership of Broadcast Stations," *Journalism Quarterly,* (Summer 1969), p. 234.

The government's concern relates particularly to the big cities and their major television stations. But, by the government's count there are only 43 cities left in which there is more than one major newspaper owner, yet every major city has three or more competing television stations (also based on FCC definitions). Judging from their own data, cross-media ownership in the cities is not the nation's most pressing problem in the field of mass communications, regardless of the concept of the size of the market one uses.

Concern over the size of the media group is really concern over the size of the audience that it will be influencing. Implicit here is the belief that the media necessarily, willy-nilly, influence the audience. But do they? Equally perplexing is the government's view that one needs to *own* media in order to have access to the public. Do not the employees and persons who *rent* the media by buying space (newspaper) or time (broadcasting) also have an opportunity to reach the public? The important question, of course, is the extent to which owners and renters of media in fact possess the ability to influence the audience. In other words, is there *power* in the use of the mass media?

IV

Political Power

Agnewism

When, in 1970, the former Vice President of the United States, Spiro Agnew, denounced the media nearly everyone accepted his basic premise that the media had the power to "mold" public opinion. Almost no one bothered to investigate the truthfulness of this basic premise, least of all the media professionals who probably found this imputation of power a source of pride. Instead, the question that was debated was whether the media were being fair in their use of this power.

"Molding" public opinion can be interpreted in one of two ways: that the public is malleable because it accepts what it is told; or that it sits in judgment on the information it receives and uses it to form its opinions. The distinction is critical. It is the difference between imputing ignorance or intelligence to the audience. Agnew's use of the term implied that the audience is malleable and ignorant—otherwise why be so concerned? Misrepresentation of the facts is easily dealt with.

Eventually, the truth will out (as Agnew himself was destined to learn).

Agnew expressed the administration's indignation at being subjected to criticism, fearing that the public's attitude had been prejudiced. But unjustified as the criticism might or might not have been, the administration certainly did not want for access to the American mind. Virtually all of the media were at its disposal in order to debate the issues. Indeed in his first 18 months in office President Nixon appeared on television as many times as Presidents Eisenhower, Kennedy and Johnson combined.[1]

In addition, the administration has at its disposal the enormous power of the federal bureaucracy. In Dale Minor's *The Information of War*, the public information operations of the executive branch were said to cost the taxpayer $400 million a year, or more than double the cost of newsgathering by the two major U.S. wire services, the three major television networks, and the ten largest newspapers in the United States combined.[2]

In addition to Nixon's unlimited ability to make his views known to the public on his own terms by commandeering the nation's entire broadcasting establishment and by being able to put into the field a veritable army of public relations men, his critics in the news media have a public relations problem of their own. An ABC Network poll following Agnew's attack on the broadcast media found that 51 percent of the public agreed with him that the media were biased, 16 percent were uncertain and 33 percent disagreed.[3] This is not a picture of a public that is unaware of the quality of its news sources. Why then were Agnew and the president so exercised about their treatment by the mass media?

With time it has become apparent that they could have been concerned that the probing of reporters might have revealed what was eventually revealed, the unseemly behavior that led to Agnew's resignation and brought Nixon to the brink of impeachment. But Nixon's known attitude toward the mass media tends to support the likelihood that he truly accepts the myth of the public's credulousness. That, as he sees it, the mass media determine his personal popularity and the success or failure of his policies. If this is true then it is understandable that he should fear any negativism in the mass media, particularly if he is of the opinion, as Agnew stated it, that there is a conspiracy against him among the "liberal eastern establishment."

Getting the Facts

Congressman Robert Eckhardt (Dem., Texas) made a rare attempt to test Agnew's assertion that the "liberal eastern establishment" were implacably hostile to the Nixon administration. He took upon himself the task of surveying the editorial policies of 154 newspapers and their views on a number of key political issues that preoccupied the Nixon administration in the 1968-1970 period.

The greatest opposition to administration policies, it was found, came from the Midwestern papers, not those in the ("liberal") East. Perhaps equally surprising, the greatest support came from the Western papers rather than the Southern. As a matter of fact, Southern newspaper responses were not at all different from responses of newspapers as a whole.

Carswell's nomination to the Supreme Court had little editorial support, even in the South; the Eastern press was not the radical liberal monolith that the Vice President thought it was; and any opposition that there was in the press to administration policies was not part of a liberal conspiracy. The administration, when it lost a majority of the large newspapers on an issue, lost by and large its basic supporters. Two-thirds of the nation's newspapers *endorsed* Nixon-Agnew in 1968 but 69 percent *opposed* Carswell, 65 percent were upset by the Vice President's statements on war dissenters, and only half the press supported the Cambodian operations.

The Eckhardt study showed that the newspapers are Republican-oriented but apparently they are not slaves to the party and its leaders' policies. They can and do provide a platform for diverse editorial positions on questions of important national policy.

The Republican party received the endorsement of the majority of the newspapers in every election since 1932 with the exception of 1964. Their margin has been two or three to one over the Democratic candidate and in terms of the newspapers' circulation, rather than the number of newspapers, it was often higher.

The survey also revealed that both in the Northeast, whose "liberal press" was attacked so vehemently by the Vice President, as well as in the traditionally Democratic South, the Republican presidential candidate generally had the support of the majority of the newspapers.

In attacking the press for allegedly failing to support administration policies, Agnew clearly implied that the absence of public support on some issues must necessarily mean that the media were failing him, in other words, that the public's mind had not been properly conditioned by them.

The difficulties facing the Nixon administration were thus being blamed on the public's "informers," that is the media, rather than on the events that made the electorate unhappy: the depressing, spirit-rending stories of over a decade of war, death, riots, and finally corruption. These were not the fault of the media, unless one would argue that the public should not be informed.

What could have caused Agnew (and Nixon) to be so misled? The evidence indicates that the idea that the media are intrinsically powerful (i.e., influential) probably is one of the few ideas that the media have truly been able to impose on the public. Writing in his own newspaper, Richard Harwood, a managing editor of the *Washington Post* (among the most prominent of the so-called Eastern Establishment newspapers; its parent company also owns *Newsweek* magazine, as well as several television and radio stations and a wire service), quoted Walter Lippmann to the effect that there is a "realization in this country that the power to shape the mass mind. . .has fallen into the hands of a very small number of men and women [journalists] . . . .They are the new Popes in their influence on the secular mind in America."[4] Similarly, Fred Friendly, formerly head of CBS News and now head of the Columbia University School of Journalism, calls television a "potent magic wand."[5] This type of self-inflating professionalism is analogous to Hollywood's penchant for making films of the lives of entertainers, or the church's canonization of clerics. Professional narcissism is more responsible for concern regarding the power of the media than their ability truly to manipulate the public mind.

A close look at specific media in specific markets where political power can be suspected was undertaken by the author a few years ago. It focused on the question of whether or not the media "mold" public opinion. A cross sectional view of findings in three cities follows.

Chicago: The Big City Baron

Chicago, the third largest city in the nation, has that combination of circumstances that calls attention to the role of the mass media. It has a powerful mayor-boss, Richard Daley, one of the few left in America's major cities, but paradoxically it is also one of the few major cities with two strong competing media groups: McCormick-Patterson and Field Enterprises (Marshall Field).

The McCormick-Patterson group owns a local AM and FM radio station, a popular local television station (WGN), and two of Chicago's four principal newspapers: *The Chicago Tribune*, which has a morning circulation within the City of Chicago of 305,000, and *Chicago Today*, which has an evening circulation within the city of 287,000. Together the corporation's two newspapers reach 51 percent of the households in the city every day. When its other media are included, the McCormick-Patterson group probably reaches every home in Chicago in the course of an average week.

Field Enterprise's holdings in Chicago also consist of two newspapers: the *Chicago Sun Times* (338,000 within the city) and the *Chicago Daily News* (245,000) and a small local television station (WFLD). Like McCormick-Patterson, the Field Enterprise's two newspapers reach almost half of Chicago's households. However, in the course of an average week it is not as likely that Field's media reach most of the local citizenry because of the relatively smaller size of its television audience.

The three network television and radio stations in Chicago are also dominant, in that they reach every Chicago home in the course of an average week. But there are also a great number of smaller media in Chicago—402 different media originate in the greater Chicago area, owned by 224 different companies or groups, and another 80 different media, owned by 55 different owners, enter the market from outside.[6] However, with the exception of network television and radio stations and a number of nationally distributed magazines, none share anywhere near the popularity of the McCormick-Patterson or Field Enterprise groups. And the exceptions don't really count since network-owned media as well as nationally distributed magazines rarely become embroiled in local politics.

To test the influence of the McCormick-Patterson group in Chicago, the author made an analysis of its political endorsements during the local primary and subsequent municipal elections in 1967. It was found that of 56 local political contests the two McCormick-Patterson newspapers endorsed opposing candidates in half of them. Both of the McCormick-Patterson newspapers, however, supported Mayor Daley.

Of the candidates endorsed by the *Chicago Tribune*, only 50 percent won in the primaries, and 57 percent in the elections. The other newspaper of the McCormick-Patterson group, *Chicago Today*, did better—82 percent of the candidates it endorsed won in the primaries and 80 percent in the elections. With the exception of Mayor Daley these media went in different directions and scored differently as a result.

The election of endorsed candidates should be interpreted with care. It does not necessarily prove media influence. Did the media succeed in selling the public on those candidates or did it merely succeed in reading the public mind? Mayor Daley is a case in point. Is his success since 1955 to be attributed to the support he obtained from the media, to his opponents' ineptitude, to his own political organization's ability to turn out the vote, or to his own ability? These are not simple questions. It is almost certain, however, that the dominant media are not the basis of Mayor Daley's political power.

The two newspapers of the other major newspaper group in Chicago, the Field Enterprises, endorsed the same candidates and were more successful than the McCormick-Patterson organization. More than 89 percent of their endorsed candidates won. Did the more successful Field Enterprise group influence the public while the McCormick-Patterson group failed? Or is the Field group simply more in tune with the public's attitudes?

If this problem isn't tantalizing enough, we can always return to the first question, the paradox that Chicago has one of the few political bosses left in America, yet is one of the very few cities which still has competing dailies as well as a plethora of other media.

Atlanta's Cox: No Control

In Atlanta, Georgia, the nation's eighteenth largest communications market, there is considerably less competition, compared to Chicago. The Cox organization owns the only two major dailies in Atlanta, as well as one of the city's major television and radio stations (WSB). Unlike Chicago, which boasts nine local television stations, Atlanta has only five. Cox's media properties reach into every home in the market and face serious competition from only two of the other four television stations in the city.

In 1968, Cox's television station, WSB, commissioned a study of political attitudes among its viewers. They found that nearly 75 percent of the registered voters in the state watched WSB's programs and that 91 percent of them could identify Hal Suit, the stations's newscaster, when they were shown his picture. (Hal Suit subsequently put this public exposure to political advantage by winning the Republican nomination for governor, although he lost to the Democratic candidate in the election.)

Yet despite Cox's formidable position in Atlanta, the following description of the city's mayoral election in 1969 provides a striking illustration of the dubious role of media in directing public opinion.

The long time and popular Democratic mayor of Atlanta, Ivan Allen, Jr., had retired and threw his support to his vice mayor Samuel Massell, a Jew. Massell ran against the Republican alderman, Rodney Cook, a white Protestant. On the Sunday before the election the Cox media carried news of an alleged shakedown of local nightclub owners, by Massell's brother and a detective on the Atlanta police force, for political contributions to support Massell. As a result, Allen shifted his support from Massell to Cook and even went so far as to publicly request Massell to withdraw from the election. All the while, Cox's newspapers pressed hard for Cook and attacked Massell vigorously.

Result: Massell won overwhelmingly, by 61,000 votes over Cook's 49,000.

The inability of the Cox organization to influence a local election despite its formidable array of local media, a major issue, the turn-around support of a popular local leader, and a possible religious bias, cannot be attributed to ineptitude. The president of the Cox organization is J. Leonard Reinsch, the national media consultant to the Democratic party.

Nor could Massell's success be written off as a Southern kneejerk reflex favoring Democrats over Republicans. In the gubernatorial elections, Republican candidate Calloway received 425,000 votes to Democrat Lester Maddox's

420,000. (In the absence of a clear majority the choice was up to the Georgia Legislature, which chose Maddox.)

Despite the dominant position of the Cox organization in Atlanta, their media were less successful in endorsing eventual winners in local elections than were the Field Enterprises in Chicago, where media competition is more intense. Thus, in 1968, the *Atlanta Journal* was 61 percent successful and the *Atlanta Constitution*, 53 percent. (In 1969, their scores improved to 66 percent and 81 percent, respectively.) It might be noted in passing that the two Cox newspapers did not agree on the endorsement of 30 percent of the local issues and local candidates, though this does not explain their inability to influence the local mayoral election, where both Cox newspapers were in agreement.

Southern Gentility: Meridian, Mississippi

Now let's look at a market that is as nearly sewed-up by one media owner as it is possible to be. Meridian, Mississippi, represents the hoariest example of media dominance that could be found among America's 204 markets. The Meridian market as a whole (which covers ten surrounding counties) includes 76,300 homes. In population it ranks 151st of 204 markets in the United States (the 204th is the smallest market). Meridian had, in 1970, only one media owner, Mrs. James H. Skewes, whose properties could reach nearly all of the homes in the market. With no real competition, the potential for domination in Meridian is high.

Thus, the town's only daily newspaper, the *Meridian Star*, with a circulation of 22,527, is owned by Mrs. James H. Skewes, and operated by her son, James B. Skewes. The

Skewes are also the sole owners of the market's most widely listened to AM radio station and have an 11 percent interest in the town's only television station, WTOK, whose shares are widely held. The station carries programs from two networks (CBS and ABC) and is credited by the ARB, the audience rating firm, with 68 percent of the local audience.

Competition from other local media is weak. The next closest local competitor to the Skewes interests is radio station WOKK, owned by the New South Broadcasting Company, but it reaches only 15 percent of the market's homes. There is another television station in Meridian: WHTV, a UHF station broadcasting on Channel 24. It also carries programs from two networks (NBC and ABC) but has a very small share of the market.

As for newspapers, the only competition facing the Skewes *Meridian Star* comes from the *Jackson Clarion-Ledger* and the *Birmingham News* (but both of these papers reach less than 4 percent of the market). Most people in Meridian get most of their news from the Skewes interests. The potential for domination clearly is present. The question is how do the Skeweses use this potential? Prior to the mayoral primaries and general elections of June 1969, the *Star*'s editorials did not endorse any candidate for any office.

While it is true that Meridian does not yet seem to be the beneficiary of the two-party system, it is still possible that there were some significant issues which could have been raised for debate when a city of 50,000 approached city council elections. But the local media aired none.

In the November 1968 national elections the *Star* did half-heartedly endorse Nixon for President noting that "Our hearts are with Wallace, but he probably has no chance of winning."

The substantial local business interests of the media stock-holders in Meridian may partly account for this reluctance to stimulate local debate. But another explanation lies in the political environment itself. It is reasonably safe to take sides on issues over which people are divided, even if your business depends on their continued public patronage. But it is not so safe when most people are known to hold strong and basically identical views.

In effect, the situation in Meridian illustrates the passive role of local small town media owners. Politically colorless or at best adopting the community's outlook, they hardly provide the type of local service envisaged by the FCC when it created a system of local television broadcasters. Often as not, the dominant media owners in small towns do not dominate, they merely plod.

Even though there is no serious competition from media outside the market, it is doubtful that the public in small markets like Meridian would ever be the political captives of the local media owner. In small markets the local political leaders are generally familiar figures to practically every family in the area. There is no need for local political candidates in small communities to rely on television, or any other medium for that matter, in order to obtain exposure to their electorate.

In large metropolitan areas, on the other hand, the situation more nearly resembles the national model, where the public relies on the media for knowledge of its political leaders. Here, however, there are compensating forces at work. In the major markets, where there is in fact greater political reliance on the media, the intense competition among the several dominant media owners (defined as those able to reach nearly every home), is generally sufficient to prevent their dominant position from being translated into real political power. This can be seen in the fact that political bossism in the major markets has been confined to the history books. The substantial strides in the development of

mass communications in recent years have not been accompanied by the entrenchment of political power but by an
increase in its instability, for reasons we will examine shortly.

Political Advertising

Thus far we have discussed the political role of the *owners* of
the mass media. But in the United States the ability to use
the mass communications facilities for political purposes is
not restricted to its owners. Anyone may "rent" the media to
advance the cause of a candidate or an issue, through the
purchase of newspaper space or air time. This, of course,
makes even more suspect the great concern of the government regarding media ownership. Indeed, the accessibility of
the mass media to those who can afford to pay the price is
possibly a more serious social and political issue than is media
ownership.

The broadcast media, particularly television, have brought
into the political arena an increasing number of people who
in the past could not have stood for public office without
either winning the support of the old-line party machines or
fighting them. Television and radio (and computerized mailings) have enabled them to go directly to the people over the
heads of the political machines.

While this has opened politics to fresh talent and introduced a new political style, it also has its problems: it may
eventually restrict political activity to the wealthy. Initially,
however, it has rendered unstable whatever power had been
possessed by local political organizations and local media
owners.

The total cost of political campaigning has leaped. The
Citizens' Research Foundation estimates that between 1964
and 1968, total political spending by all candidates at all

levels increased 50 percent from $200 million in 1964 to $300 million in 1968 (both presidential election years). This has drawn attention away from the old problems of political machines and bossism, and focused concern on the use of mass media for political campaigning. In fact, however, of the $300 million spent in political campaigning in 1968, only $58.9 million was spent by all candidates for air time on television and radio in *both* the primaries and the general elections. In 1972, (also a presidential election year) the FCC reports that nearly the same sum—$59.3 million, was spent by all candidates for television and radio in the primaries and general elections combined (see Table 7). The broadcast media thus accounted for a relatively small and stable part of the cost of political campaigning.

At the national level, as shown below, the greater part of the exposure of presidential candidates on the broadcast media was obtained *free*. Thus in 1972, 85 percent of the network air time used by the presidential candidates was obtained without charge.[7] Nevertheless, many hold to the myth that the use of the mass media is responsible for the high cost of political campaigning.

It is also interesting to note that from the standpoint of television, political advertising is a very minor source of revenue. The three television networks, for example, received

TABLE 7

Radio and Television Revenue from Political Advertising—1972
(Millions of Dollars)

	TOTAL	TELEVISION		RADIO	
		NETWORKS	STATIONS	NETWORKS	STATIONS
Primaries	$21.4	$ —	$12.5	$ —	$ 8.8
Elections	37.9	4.8	19.6	0.5	13.0
Total	$59.3	$4.8	$32.1	$0.5	$21.8

Source: *FCC Report On Political Broadcasting (1973)*

a combined total of only $4.8 million from all the primaries and general elections held in 1972. By comparison, network advertising revenues from all sources in 1972 totaled $1.4 billion.

Of the total revenue of $4.8 million received for political broadcasting by the three television networks, $2.4 million consisted of large blocks of time for political programs such as telethons, film specials, or speeches. The remaining $2.4 million represented receipts from "spot" political advertisements.

All told, only 18 hours of program time were purchased from the networks by the presidential candidates. In addition, and probably more important from the standpoint of its effectiveness, the three networks together provided them with 81 hours of free time on commercially sponsored programs such as *Issues and Answers*, *Face the Nation*, and the *Today Show*, plus another 21 free hours of nationwide network exposure, a total of 102 free hours in the 1972 presidential year (exclusive of network news). Altogether the presidential candidates had free nationwide exposure for the equivalent of more than an hour a day for the 14 weeks between the party conventions and the November elections.[8]

This is a considerable volume of nationwide exposure, especially when it is remembered that the networks are but one part of broadcasting. There are also the local broadcasting stations and of course the regular network news coverage through which an adroit presidential campaigner can maintain almost continuous contact with the nation without charge.

Actually, political advertising on national (network) television accounted for only 8 percent of the grand total of $59.3 million spent for air-time by all political candidates in 1972. The rest of the money, or 92 percent, went directly to the television stations ($32 million) and radio stations ($22 million), most of it into local spot announcements of 60 seconds or less. For the local television broadcasters, whose revenues from all sources totaled $1.8 billion in 1972, the $32 million received from political advertising was also a minor item.

The large number of free hours shown in Table 8 for radio stations (13,673) represents the donation of time by 5,100 broadcasters. It averages about 2.6 hours per station. The nation's 700 commercial television stations donated 2,545 hours, an average of about 3.6 hours per station.

TABLE 8

Free Radio and Television Time Provided For
Political Advertising—1972
(In Hours)

		STATIONS		NETWORKS	
	TOTAL	TELEVISION	RADIO	TELEVISION	RADIO
Primaries	6,899	1,068	5,724	73	34
Elections	9,474	1,477	7,949	29	19
Total	16,373	2,545	13,673	102	53

Source: *FCC Report On Political Broadcasting* (1973)

Equal Time

Possibly even more free station time and free network time would have been made available in the absence of Regulation 315 which is generally referred to as the *equal time rule*. This rule prohibits station licensees from selling paid time or granting free time to one candidate unless an equal amount of time is offered on the same terms to all candidates competing for the same office. Until 1959, this rule also applied to news reports, documentaries, and interviews.

In 1960 the rule was temporarily suspended to facilitate the Kennedy-Nixon debates, which explains the substantial number of free hours of nationwide network time donated to the candidates that year. If the rule had not been suspended, equal time would have had to be given to all the splinter-party candidates. The cost to the networks of the time donated to the four Kennedy-Nixon debates alone exceeded $2 million.

The equal time rule has not been suspended since 1960. It is likely that some of the candidates themselves wanted to see the rule kept so that they might avoid a public debate; Richard Nixon probably did not want to have to repeat his 1960 experience. If, however, free time had been provided without suspending the equal time rule the 1968 debators would have had to include Reverend Hensley of the Universal Party; Eldridge Cleaver of the Peace and Freedom Party; Dick Gregory of the New Party; and Bishop Tomlinson of the Theocratic Party. As it was, these parties had the right to buy air time of the type and duration paid for by the two major parties. Their financial inability to take advantage of this right effectively foreclosed their ability to use nationwide television. In 1972, the absence of these splinter parties facilitated the granting of a substantial number of free hours on national television.

A major shortcoming of nearly all the recommendations regarding political use of the media has been that they focus on the cost of air time on network television, which is a relatively minor cost and one borne only by the presidential candidates. The high cost of campaigning for other government offices or of using the other media have not been considered even by such prestigious groups as the Twentieth Century Fund (*Voters' Time, Campaign Costs In the Electronic Era*) and in its initial deliberations even by the U.S.

Congress. This is an example of the dangers resulting from the mythology surrounding mass communications.

The Future Cost of Campaigning

It is important to note that the rising cost of political campaigning is not attributable to increases in the price charged by the media. In fact, political ads in the mass media generally receive special discounts and, as noted earlier, their receipts remained stable over the 1968-1972 period. The problem, as we shall see, is not rising media costs but increased political spending, which in turn is the result of fundamental changes taking place in the structure of political organization in the United States.

One aspect of the problem is that the elective offices now resemble seats on the stock exchange. There are a relatively static number of elective positions at the state and federal levels and an increasing number of men who have the affluence to compete for them. This necessarily leads to an increase in the competitive cost as candidates try to outbid one another.

In the past, the political party or the local political machine was the gateway to elective office. Today, as already noted, the cost of the campaign is all that stands between an ambitious man of means and the general public. The broadcast media, particularly television, permit him to establish a familiarity in the public mind, a familiarity that has come to replace the party label that guided most voters in past generations. The political clubs are thus rapidly losing their "gatekeeper" function in political life. Then too, in the past the power of patronage attracted an army of free local labor to raise funds and ring doorbells for the club's candidates. But today, how many families will work for a political candidate in order that a brother or father be rewarded with a post office job (now no longer a patronage item) or a clerk's position at city hall?

Another factor to be considered is that today's transient populations and suburban outmigration force even the incumbents to expend considerable effort to make themselves known to their constituents at primary and election time. The result is an increasing dependence on mass media, media consultants, social scientists, opinion surveys, mass mailings and travel.

Furthermore the films and tapes used in television spot announcements and the research and consultants' fees that go into them make air time only a small part of the overall problem. Computerized mailings, billboards, and air travel are also more significant expenses. In 1968, these costs exceeded the cost of newspaper space and radio and television air-time by $228 million to the latter's $72 million. These are costly replacements for the old system of patronage and political favors—costs moreover that, in this period of weakened political clubs, must increasingly be borne by the candidate on his own.

Congress, whose members are most directly affected by these changes in the political process, has sought to bring these rising costs under control. In a very real sense, Congress has sought to prevent politics from becoming a rich man's game. The result was the Political Campaign Spending Act. The present law applies to all media and to campaign spending in general. It restricts campaign expenditures for candidates for federal offices to 10 cents per voter based on the census estimate for the number of voters in the area to be represented. Only 6 cents of this sum, however, may be spent for the use of the mass media. A minimum total expenditure of $50,000 is allowed under the new law where the number of voters is fewer than 500,000.

Compared to the actual expenditures of the 1970 Senatorial campaigns, the last to be held before the new law applied, the new law is very generous. In only five out of 32 states was more spent in the Senatorial campaign than would be allowed by the new law. The five cost overruns in 1970 were not substantial and the majority of the campaigns cost much less than the new legal limit. Thus in California the 10 cents per voter would allow campaign expenditures of $1,423,000. But in 1970 Tunney (who won) spent only $466,000 and Murphy (who lost) spent only $385,700. In Florida, the winner spent $53,900 and the loser spent $140,000; yet in Florida, the new law allows expenditures of $508,000, which is almost ten times greater than the sum actually spent by the winner.

Table 9, based on the 1970 Senatorial campaigns is of interest in that it not only compares the legal ceiling with actual expenditures, but also shows that in 14 out of 32 contests the winner spent less than the loser. And many of the big spenders were the incumbents. Thus, in Massachusetts, Edward Kennedy spent $151,500. His opponent, Spaulding, didn't even try. He spent only $14,900.

The Political Campaign Spending Act was motivated not only by the money issue but also by the fear of the "media men," the fear that with unlimited funds and the consequent ability to hire the best media talent, political know-nothings would populate the landscape. How well founded is this fear?

TABLE 9

The 1971 Legal Limits and Actual Senatorial Campaign Spending—1970

STATE	CEILING[a]	DEMOCRAT	SPENT	REPUBLICAN	SPENT
Alaska	$ 60,000	Kay	$ 34,000	Stevens*	$ 17,000
Arizona	123,000	Grossman	85,400	Fannin*	84,800
California	1,423,000	Tunney*	466,700	Murphy	385,000
Connecticut	211,000	Duffey	87,000	Weicker*	81,400
				Dodd	49,600
Delaware	60,000	Zimmerman	12,300	Roth*	13,600
Florida	518,000	Chiles*	53,900	Cramer	140,500
Hawaii	60,000	Heftel	64,900	Fong*	27,100
Illinois	756,000	Stevenson*	254,900	Smith	235,900
Indiana	350,000	Hartke*	182,700	Roudebush	353,000
Maine	66,000	Muskie*	30,800	Bishop	8,500
Maryland	271,000	Tydings	92,600	Beall*	115,900
Massachusetts	400,000	Kennedy*	151,500	Spaulding	14,900
Michigan	597,000	Hart*	140,500	Romney	45,000
Minnesota	252,000	Humphrey*	158,000	McGregor	166,900
Missouri	322,000	Symington*	192,200	Danforth	231,500
Montana	60,000	Mansfield*	10,600	Wallace	10,200
Nebraska	100,000	Morrison	21,600	Hruska*	26,500
Nevada	60,000	Cannon*	68,100	Raggio	73,800
		Williams*	179,900	Gross	301,500
New Mexico	63,000	Montoya*	35,500	Carter	27,600
New York	1,271,000	Ottinger	648,500	Goodell	570,400
				Buckley*	522,400
North Dakota	60,000	Burdick*	44,800	Kleppe	71,500
Ohio	716,000	Metzenbaum	238,500	Taft*	220,500
Pennsylvania	812,000	Sesler	25,000	Scott*	286,600
Rhode Island	67,000	Pastore*	16,400	McLaughlin	3,300
Tennessee	271,000	Gore	145,600	Brock*	173,400
Texas	760,000	Benten*	174,700	Bush	292,700
Utah	67,000	Moss*	115,300	Burton	91,400
Vermont	60,000	Hoff	69,700	Prouty*	53,600
Virginia	320,000	Rawlings	26,200	Garland	31,400
				Byrd*	91,900
West Virginia	117,000	Byrd*	8,100	Dodson	1,900
Wisconsin	295,000	Proxmire*	41,100	Erikson	14,400
Wyoming	60,000	McGee*	47,600	Wold	38,700

[a]Sixty percent of the ceiling may be spent on mass media.
*The winning candidate.

Source: *Broadcasting Magazine,* May 17, 1971
Senate Report (S382) 1971, p.75

Confessions of a Media Man

It used to be said that the opponent won because he had a better political machine. Today the popular notion is that the winning candidate's media man was more effective in manipulating the techniques of mass communications, implying that the winner was better at conning the electorate.

A case study of the 1970 gubernatorial election in Michigan, as reported by the winning candidate's media man, Professor Walter DeVries, sheds some light on the media man's thinking. DeVries, in a lecture at the Conference on Strategies in the New Politics held at the University of Maryland (December 1970) described his methodology as being based on two-way communication with the electorate.

First, he showed statistically that his client, Governor William Milliken, should *not* have won the election. In other statewide contests in that election the Republican vote was only 40 percent. Furthermore, his client supported two of three amendments to the state constitution each of which lost 60-40, and he opposed the third which carried 60-40. Nevertheless, Governor Milliken received 50.7 percent of the vote. How was this managed?

DeVries first sought to establish communication with the electorate by constant polling. It was found that in the last three weeks of the campaign the public's concern shifted from social issues to economic issues. Had constant polling not been employed, this would not have been acknowledged in the campaign and might well have cost them the election.

With a thumb on the public's pulse, the method of responding to the public's polled attitudes was through news channels. As the incumbent, Milliken had an advantage in this regard which he exploited. DeVries felt that television was the more important news medium. Thus, the Governor had his own cameraman covering his campaign. Almost daily, clips of 30 to 60 seconds were sent to 14 television stations throughout the state. These clips looked like news film and had some news content. Outside of Detroit, Milliken received better than 60 percent coverage. A similar technique was used for radio. In this way the candidate tapped the credibility associated with news and obtained free air-time.

To further the newsmaking technique, the Governor used press conferences rather than appearances before large audiences. At these conferences he employed audio-visual materials such as slides, charts and statistical tables, which also made news.

His television commericals were similarly designed as miniature documentaries, and focused on a few issues. They were designed to give the impression of personal competence rather than the promise of panaceas.

DeVries' candidate abandoned principle for the public will. He claims that

> [the] ideal (perfect) way to campaign (or govern) is to have a near flawless, up-to-date, two-way communications system between the candidate and the voters and the capability to respond to the information inputs. . . . . There is nothing Machiavellian about asking what problems bother people, or asking what they think ought to be done about these problems. Once I find that out, I don't think it Machiavellian to find the best media to inform people what the candidate intends to do or not do about those problems. . . . In short, campaigning (and governing) is an information and communications system.

Something new is clearly evolving to replace the party label, but is it an improvement? The new approach seems to be based in large part on opinion polls. If this approach is used only for campaign purposes, "to tell them what they want to hear," how will the public be able to judge what the candidate will do in office? Instead of giving them his own views, it is as if he looked over their shoulder and fed back to them their own views.

This new type of candidate may be a sincere technocrat seeking to implement the public will, but then, too, he may be an irresponsible opportunist without a political party's concern for continuity to act as a secondary control once he is in office.

These problems are not likely to be solved before they are first laid out on the table and their parts properly identified; least of all, if television is attributed with mystical qualities. What we are today faced with is an integrated process that incorporates a number of techniques and technologies that have been around for a while. Their integrated use is now being put to political advantage by all candidates. No one ignores them. The question is not whether one candidate's media man will find the magic formula before the other candidate's media man. Rather, the question is whether the process of so-called two-way communication doesn't contain within it a fundamental flaw.

On the other hand, there is much to be said for the concept of maintaining a two-way stream of information between the governing and the governed. Events, issues, and attitudes do change more rapidly today as the public receives information of greater variety and volume than in the past. Pragmatism is a strong tradition in American political life, and the new politics seems to be elevating it to the level of a principle.

Most important, however, in the process described above it is the views of the political candidate that are being "molded" by the public *and not the reverse.* Those who have engaged in political activity have always known this fact of life. Thus, the zest with which the politicians and bureaucrats approach the task of protecting the public interest in communications matters conceals their more fundamental motivation, concern for the effect of the media on those in the public limelight—on themselves.

V

The Government and the Media

Fear of the Tube

The federal government regulates railroads, trucks, airlines, natural gas, electric power, and the banks, but the politicians and bureaucrats are most concerned about the mass media, particularly television. More testimony, press releases and threats to our constitutional rights followed from an otherwise not so impressive CBS program *The Selling of the Pentagon*, than from the power breakdown which blacked out the entire Northeast, the bankruptcy of the Penn Central Railroad, soaring interest rates, or the worst plane crash. The reason for this is fairly apparent. The politician and the bureaucrat fear any exposure, however benign, that in any way examines the premises and processes that underly public policy. *The Selling of the Pentagon* simply described how the Department of Defense spent taxpayers' money promoting its own view of foreign policy, something most informed persons knew was being done, although it was improper.

The FCC investigated the complaints of some Congressmen filed against CBS for its *Pentagon* program and found no basis for citing the network for violation of the Communications Act.

But Representative Staggers, Chairman of the Subcommittee on Communications, would not let go. He pressed CBS to disclose its outtakes from the *Pentagon* program for reasons discussed in the next chapter. When CBS refused, his subcommittee cited the network and its officers for contempt of Congress. The House of Representatives as a whole voted against such a citation. As one journalist posed the issue: Suppose *The Selling of the Pentagon* had been a newspaper article? It would probably have generated an irate letter to the editor, but not much more. And if issue were taken with a newspaper article, it would go through the courts, as was the case in the printing of the Pentagon's Vietnam papers by the *New York Times* and *Washington Post*.

The awe with which the politicians and bureaucrats look upon television is based on the myth that it possesses an unusual ability to influence the public, as if the information being transmitted was secondary, and the medium itself possessed power. The fact that TV's *The Selling of the Pentagon* aroused little public interest, despite two rebroadcasts, while newspaper publication of the Pentagon Papers had an immense impact did not alter the government's fear of television nor its relative equanimity toward the press.

By keeping close tabs on the FCC, which is the licensing authority, Congress maintains a more credible threat to the broadcasting industry (especially television which is feared the most) than if it kept the FCC at arm's length as it does the other regulatory agencies. For this reason, the trade press and Washington attorneys representing broadcasters earn handsome incomes by keeping a sharp eye on the FCC-Congressional symbioses in order to guide and inform the industry regarding the forces at work in the politically sensitive field of mass communications.

Congressional Control

A study of the behavior of Congress and its relationship to the FCC by Krasnow and Longley concluded that although major laws affecting the communications industry are rarely enacted, Congress nonetheless exerts a very significant influence on the regulatory agency and on the industry by means of investigations, public hearings, executive sessions, committee reports, and "requests for information."[1]

During a Congressional hearing of the FCC, committee members have an opportunity to communicate their views to a captive audience of FCC commissioners who usually try to portray themselves as flexible, hard-working members of a public-spirited agency. In addition, informal oversight activities take place before and after such hearings.

When Newton Minow called upon Speaker Sam Rayburn shortly after his appointment to the FCC, in 1961, Mr. Sam put his arm around the new FCC Chairman and said, "Just remember one thing, son. Your agency is an arm of the Congress, you belong to us. Remember that and you'll be all right." The FCC commissioners and staff have long been aware of this fact of life, as they spend much of their time attempting to perceive and anticipate the attitudes of key congressmen and committees. This process, which has been referred to by political scientists as "anticipated reaction," "feedback," or "strategic sensitivity," is an important element in the exercise of congressional authority over the FCC.

More recently, however, it has taken second place to a new—and more powerful—force on the media scene.

Attack by the President

The executive branch of government has recently exhibited an active (and unprecedented) interest in mass communications. The traditional method of exercising presidential influence had been through speeches and press conferences, which frequently preempt broadcasts in prime time. Even in lower-keyed activities the President is certain to make the evening news reports. In either case, his principal objective is to influence the public by direct exposure of his views. This has more recently led to tension between the president and the networks, since the networks analyze Presidential statements immediately after they're made, with a nationwide audience sometimes learning both sides of a political issue. In an environment unusually anxious regarding the power of the media, and with a strong executive in the White House, it was inevitable that the two should come into conflict.

The executive branch embarked on its war with the media first by employing the Vice President to denounce specific communications companies as described in Chapter IV. This "jawboning" was designed to activate the license syndrome, the fear among broadcasters and networks that they might face unusual problems at license renewal time. It has been known to be effective.

A more sophisticated approach was to use the media itself. The Executive Office of Communications employs the press release with particular skill especially in reaching small-town newspapers. The presidential support staff most directly involved in public policy in the field of mass communications, however, is the Office of Telecommunications Policy (OTP). For a small office with ill-defined objectives, it has a rather big budget of close to $3 million a year, plus several million dollars of Commerce Department funds appropriated for its Telecommunications Policy Division.

Established in 1970, the tasks of OTP were vaguely defined. In its first two years, practically every interview with its director, Dr. Clay T. Whitehead, included a question regarding his duties. By 1973, however, he began to define its purposes in a way that can only be described as the development of a mini-FCC, or the President's FCC, as contrasted with the congressional FCC discussed earlier.

During the election campaign of 1972, when Senator George McGovern and his ill-starred choice for Vice President, Senator Eagleton, were being drubbed by the media, the White House was respectfully silent on communications matters. But the honeymoon was shortlived. Early in 1973 the OTP launched a major campaign against the three television networks.

Let's Get 'Em

Instead of employing the criticism of the type delivered by the Vice President a year or two earlier, OTP prepared the communications industry for radical surgery. The plan was (and still is) to separate the broadcasters from the networks and use the former as a control over the latter.

To win over the broadcasting affiliates of the networks, Whitehead proposed legislation (in the name of the White House) that would ease the concerns of television station owners at license renewal time. Thus, he proposed lengthening the term of the license from three years to five. Regarding challenges to renewing the license, the FCC would be required to find that an incumbent's record did not merit renewal before it could designate the renewal for hearing. The proposed law would also bar the FCC from restructuring the industry on a case-by-case basis (which is how Boston's WHDH lost its license).

But the White House also named its price for this legislation which broadcasters had long desired. Clay Whitehead called upon the broadcasters to exercise "control" over the news coming from the television networks. And, as pointed out by Leonard Zeidenberg in an article in *Broadcasting* magazine, Whitehead let the industry know, in no uncertain terms, that it would punish those whom it felt did not treat news "objectively." As Whitehead put it: "Station managers and network officials who fail to act to correct imbalance or consistent bias from the networks—or who acquiesce by silence—can only be considered willing participants, to be held fully accountable by the broadcaster's community at license renewal time."[2]

To put life into this threat, at about this time, local conservatives in Florida challenged the renewal of the licenses of two Post-Newsweek television stations.[3] Rumor had it that some of these groups were encouraged by, if not actually operating on, the advice of the White House.

Interestingly, it was the staff of the Jacksonville, Florida station owned by the Post-Newsweek organization that brought to light facts that led the Senate to reject the nomination of Harold Carswell to the Supreme Court. Equally significant, it was the subsequent investigative efforts of two *Washington Post* staffers that created a national issue out of the Watergate affair.

Patrick Buchanan, who edits a daily digest of press and broadcast news stories for the President every morning, indicated in an interview for a *New York Times Magazine* article why the White House staff was particularly concerned about television. "In terms of *power over the American people*, you can't compare newspapers to those pictures on television. They can make or break a politician. It's all over if you get chopped up on the networks. You can never recover."[4] Again the fear of the power of the media to *manipulate* its audience was motivating public policy, despite the fact that Richard Nixon himself survived such a "chopping up" to become President of the United States.

Attack by the Judiciary

At about the same time that the executive branch began to move aggressively against the mass media, the judicial branch sent a bolt through the industry in the now famous Caldwell decision which denied a *New York Times* reporter (Earl Caldwell) immunity from revealing his sources of information when subpoenaed by a federal court.

Within weeks of the Caldwell decision, there followed a number of attempts to get newsmen to identify confidential news sources. Several went to jail. Reporters were also arrested and convicted for receiving and printing the contents of government documents obtained without authorization. In some instances, judges ordered the press to refrain from making public certain information in connection with criminal trials so as not to influence the jury. The barred information, however, included a jury verdict, the names of witnesses, testimony in open court, and the criminal records of defendants.

Thus, with its reliability as a source of information long since compromised by misuse of the "secret" stamp and the dissemination of false information, the government now seeks to constrain the mass media from probing for the truth. With reporters no longer immune from subpoena, reliable informants will be reluctant to pass information on to them.

Dissenters, in and out of the establishment, now no longer have the means of bringing otherwise secret events, plans, and policies to the public's view. This includes disgruntled military men, diplomats, police, Black Panthers, Wall Street executives, and drug pushers. We will never know what this loss of confidentiality will cost because we will never know what we might have known.

Public affairs are gradually becoming the exclusive preserve of the bureaucracy and of a small group of temporarily appointed and elected officials. Even the current attempt by Congress to write a law that will return to the media some modicum of immunity from subpoena is itself a loss of freedom. By defining the limits of freedom of the press, Congress is now in a position to limit it. A major American tradition has been violated by each of the three branches of the government. It is unlikely that this damage can be repaired. In the Caldwell decision alone, America has taken a major step away from being the open society it once was.

Surprises

As we have seen, the operation of the nation's mass communications system, television in particular, is surrounded by a wide array of pressure groups. These include the FCC, Congress, the President, the Justice Department, the Pentagon, savvy attorneys, public interest groups, the networks, broadcasters, and cable television industry, their respective trade associations, and individual large corporations. It is not surprising that all these cooks lead to generally dull fare.

Indeed it is a wonder, with all this overseeing and contesting, that television manages to produce a number of fairly spicy dishes each year. By contrast, the printed media, which are wholly unregulated and almost untouchable in this regard, are, (as a consequence) much more consistently controversial and exciting in their content. Nevertheless, they cause much less of a furor. The explanation is that whatever a single newspaper, magazine, or book may report, unless it is picked up and broadcasted by the television networks, it reaches too few people to be a political threat. In large part, this protects the printed media from government interference as much as does the First Amendment.

The way in which the anti-trust laws are applied to the different media reflect differences in the "power" attributed to these media. Thus Congress has given special permission for the joint operation of competing newspapers in half of the 43 cities where some competition still remains. This policy was made part of Congressional legislation with the passage of the Failing Newspaper Act of 1970. In addition, tax regulations permit the accumulation of undistributed earnings free of the usual tax of 38½ percent for amounts over $120,000, *if the accumulation is for buying another property of the same type.* This tax policy has encouraged the growth of newspaper chains which today encompass most of America's major cities as shown in Table 10.[5] (Of course, the number of newspapers in a chain is not as significant as the size of the cities they serve. Thus, Hearst's eight newspapers have a combined circulation of about 2 million, while Freedom's 20 newspapers have a combined circulation of about 400,000).

In the broadcasting field, on the other hand, the FCC limited radio and television groups to just seven stations in each medium.

In general, the government's official treatment of the different types of media differs, based on assumptions regard-

TABLE 10
Major Newspaper Chains—1970

CHAIN	NO. OF NEWSPAPERS OWNED
Scripps League	29
Gannet	27
Newhouse	23
Cowles-Ridder	23
Thomson	23
E. W. Scripps	20
Freedom	20
Lee	18
Stauffer	13
Knight	11
Cox	11
Hearst	8
McCormick	7

Source: *Broadcasting Yearbook* (1970)

ing their influence with the public. In all probability, if television stations were not functioning as conduits for nationwide networks, but were programmed independently in each market, as was originally intended by the FCC, they would be less feared by the government. However, the forces of the marketplace have circumvented government policy. Thus, there are, in effect, just three "chains" in television, the three networks, though these networks are formed by business contracts rather than ownership. It doesn't really matter who owns the broadcasting stations affiliated with a network since they all carry almost the same programming anyway. Thus, the limitation on the number of broadcast stations that can be owned by a single company is not very meaningful. However, when the rules were first established the government evidently failed to anticipate the industry's pattern of development. When this pattern became evident the regulations were not changed for, as we shall see, government regulation tends to favor the status quo.

The Plan

Given the love-hate relationship between the politician (and the bureaucrat) and the mass media, particularly television, one would not expect that public policy in this field would proceed in a rational fashion. One's expectations are not disappointed.

With nearly every American community served by at least one newspaper and several radio stations, the FCC nevertheless chose to create a television system that was designed to provide more local service. As a result, most American communities have fewer than three television stations, that is, three programs, to choose from. Approximately 20 percent of the homes in the United States (48 million people) cannot receive more than two television stations. The sizes of many of the television markets designed by the FCC are simply too small to support more television broadcasting stations.

Had the FCC created a system of large regional television markets, each with a substantial number of broadcasting stations, the public would have had at its disposal a greater variety of program choices than is now the case. To some extent, this is what took place in the major cities, such as New York, Los Angeles and Chicago, where television stations established before 1949 were "grandfathered" into the system. In New York City, for example, stacked up on top of the Empire State Building, are the transmitting antennas of seven different television broadcasting stations, including one that is officially assigned to New Jersey.

If the FCC's plan had been applied to New York City, it is likely that Manhattan, Brooklyn, Queens, the Bronx, and Staten Island would each have their own television stations.

But the number of commercial stations available to the residents of each borough would have been fewer than the seven now available throughout the city. The reason is both economic and physical. In economic terms, the fewer the number of homes in the station's coverage area, the fewer the number of stations that can be supported, since the size of the audience determines the amount of advertising revenue flowing into each market. In physical terms, television stations broadcasting on the same or adjoining frequencies require considerable separation, one from the other, to prevent interference. This tends to limit the number that can be located in close proximity.

Most of the television stations on the air in New York City today cover much more than just the city itself. They are almost regional in scope. Thus, station WCBS-TV, which began operating in 1941, well before the FCC's allocation plan was even conceived, provides television service as far north as New Haven, Connecticut, as far south as Trenton, New Jersey, and westward into Allentown, Pennsylvania. The New York City television market is almost a regional market.

But in some states investors were caught unprepared. There were no television licenses granted for New Jersey or Delaware before the plan went into effect. Today there is only one commercial television station on-the-air in New Jersey, and Delaware has none at all. In both states, the majority of the viewers rely on television stations in Philadelphia and New York City for their programs. The close proximity of the population centers of New Jersey and Delaware to the powerful transmitters in Philadelphia and New York City prevented the assignment of spectrum space in these neighboring communities.

Local Service: Seed of Future Problems

For nearly two decades local service was the touchstone of government policy in the field of mass communications. Everything else was secondary. Indeed, the original FCC plan eventually led to the demise (in 1955) of the DuMont Television Network, because there weren't enough markets of significant size to support a fourth network. Had it survived, there would now be four sources of programming instead of the present three (ABC, CBS, NBC).

The FCC felt that local television stations in as many communities as possible would facilitate access to television by candidates for local political office. If a television station's signal covered too many communities, the mayor of one town would bore the viewers in neighboring towns who, understandably, would have no interest in another community's politics. This underlying objective, however, was basically unsound.

The impossibility of providing at least one television station in each political jurisdiction or even in *most* political jurisdictions is evident from a cursory glance at the figures. There are 17,105 towns; 18,048 municipalities; and 3,049 counties in the United States. The FCC's engineers could squeeze out, at most, only about 1,800 channel assignments from the spectrum space set aside for television.

Because so few channel assignments had to be spread as thinly as possible over a great many jurisdictions, many viewers are today unable to receive all three networks. The uneven geographic distribution of television stations, already described, was merely the surface effect of the Commission's allocation plan. Underneath the surface, it had an effect upon communications policy that has yet to work itself out. As shown below, the FCC's original allocation plan for television eventually led to the extension of Federal authority into intrastate communications, and even into the regulation of the manufacture of television sets.

The UHF Problem

Even though the available spectrum space allowed for only about 1,800 television stations to service over 38,000 major local jurisdictions, investors weren't interested in most of them. In fact, by 1973 only about 680 commercial television stations were on the air. The problem was that nearly 1,000 of the available station licenses were for "UHF" (Ultra High Frequency) channels 14 through 83, located on the second dial on the television set. (Channels 2 through 13 are in the "VHF"—Very High Frequency—band). UHF channels present serious problems for their investors.

To some extent the UHF problem had its origins in the four year "freeze" (1949-52) when the FCC did not license new television broadcast stations while it awaited completion by its engineers of the television allocation plan. However, all of the stations licensed before 1949 (a total of 107) broadcast on the VHF band (channels 2 through 13). Thus, during the four-year "freeze," 20 million television receivers were sold, none of which could receive UHF signals. This created a national market composed exclusively of VHF receivers.

After the four-year "freeze" on new television licenses, the Commission quickly ran out of VHF assignments. Of the approximately 120 UHF licensees who took the chance that UHF would catch on, one-quarter went off the air within twenty-four months because they had no audience. By 1949, forty-four had failed. The capital losses were substantial.

In subsequent years another dimension was added to the UHF problem. VHF television stations, being there first, were the vehicle that brought the three television networks into every major city in the nation. Most UHF broadcasters thus have to obtain their own programs, since the networks are booked-up. This means that despite poor advertising revenues due to the small markets (in other words, small audiences), most UHF broadcasters have to pay for all their own programs. By contrast, stations affiliated with a network are paid by the network to carry the network's programs.

There are also technical disadvantages to broadcasting on channels 14 through 83. UHF stations are more expensive to build than VHF stations, and the viewers have great difficulty tuning in to UHF stations. It is difficult to find the UHF station on the second dial and when successful, the picture is generally poor and the sound and color are unstable.

The system of small-town UHF stations conceived by government planners has not taken shape, lacking as it does an audience of sufficient size to support either local unaffiliated broadcast stations or a fourth network that might provide the economic support not otherwise available.

Ironically, of the small, local broadcasters that are on the air, most are *not* providing local programming. Local programs such as meetings of the town council, local garden shows, or high school basketball games, do not generally attract large audiences and therefore do not attract much advertising support. Television stations located in relatively small markets lack the financial resources necessary to contribute station time for such programs. Only broadcasters in the large urban markets can and do provide some local service of the type envisaged by the FCC, that is, other than just local news and weather and in time periods that attract audiences.

The importance of the UHF problem cannot be exaggerated. In 1972 of 164 commercial UHF stations on the air, 92 (56 percent) were losing money, and 75 of them each lost over $50,000 that year.

Solving the UHF Problem, or How the Other Dial Got There

Still hopeful of creating a system based on "local service," the FCC sought ways to encourage investment in UHF broadcasting stations. To increase the size of the UHF audience the Commission asked and received from Congress the All-Channel Bill, which banned from interstate commerce, after April 1964, all television sets that do not have an 82 channel capacity (of which 70 channels are in the UHF band). Thus, through the gradual replacement of existing television receivers, it will eventually be possible for all homes at least to receive UHF signals.

But this policy, like the original FCC plan it hoped to make effective, was not based on an economic analysis of the factors involved, such as the inherent unattractiveness of small television markets where most UHF assignments are located. Investors are not going to be enticed into setting up UHF television stations simply because UHF receivers are in every home. It is also important that the number of homes in a station's broadcast area be large enough to make the investment worthwhile.

Paradoxically, only in the large markets with their immense audiences, some numbering in the millions, may investment in UHF broadcasting stations prove attractive as more UHF sets come into operation. This, however, does not advance the cause of local service. The big cities are already very well served by substantial numbers of television stations.

But having applied the weight of government authority to the development of UHF, at considerable expense to the consumer, the FCC now must push and protect UHF development as vigorously as it first championed local service.

Each television set now costs about $15 more because of its UHF receiver components. Thus, the 70 million sets sold between 1965 and 1970 cost the public a total of about $1.2 billion more than it would have had there been no UHF. Special UHF antennas cost the public even more.

Thus, the FCC wandered from its original objective of local service into new areas of regulation unrelated to its original goal. Indeed, as described below, the FCC has ceased to champion local service through small markets, although they were originally supposed to have been the beneficiaries of the All Channel Bill and is now pushing UHF development—at the expense of television broadcasters in small markets.

The FCC now encourages investment in UHF broadcasting stations in the major cities in order to provide some benefits in return for the high cost of requiring UHF reception on all television sets. This goal has replaced local service as the driving force behind public policy in the field of television communications. The means has become the end.

Enter CATV

The Commission's desire for a system of small-town television broadcasters very early ran into conflict with the public's desire to receive all three network signals. As a result, auxiliary services supported by the public evolved. These included translators and boosters—relatively inexpensive devices that relay a television station's signal beyond its normal coverage area. The devices were used illegally by many communities for a number of years in order to bring in distant signals. Finally, in 1960, the FCC accepted them as part of the industry. By that time, there were nearly 1,000 such devices in use, serving as many communities. But this controversy merely set the stage for the CATV (Community Antenna Television) problem.

A CATV system consists of a fairly sophisticated antenna, generally located high on a tower or mountaintop near the community it is designed to serve. The master antenna can pick up distant (as well as local) television signals not otherwise obtained by rooftop antennas. This fairly expensive apparatus is constructed by a locally franchised company, which then sells the signals it picks up to the local townspeople, by connecting their television sets to a cable that runs from the giant antenna and is suspended from the telephone poles in that community.

By 1973 there were approximately 2,850 CATV systems, serving as many towns, located throughout the country. It is estimated that about 5 million homes (16 million people) subscribe to CATV services at a cost per home of about $60 a year. The average CATV system provides its subscribers with signals from about seven different television stations. Translators or boosters that preceded CATV had pulled in only one distant station. Without the service of CATV most subscribers would be able to receive, over-the-air, only one or two television signals, in some cases, none. In addition, signals received by CATV are of higher quality than those received through home antennas. This is especially important for color and UHF signals.[6]

More recent technological developments permit new CATV systems to supply as many as 20 signals to a television set at no significant additional cost to the CATV company. Since there aren't that many different signals or sources of programming available anywhere, this extra channel capacity could provide local governments and schools with nearly cost-free access to the local community. This more closely conforms to the FCC's original policy objective of local service. No less important, a nationwide, interconnected CATV network would release scarce spectrum space for other uses.

But CATV poses problems as well. CATV has thrived principally in small, underserved communities. The underserved markets, by definition, do not receive more than two TV signals. When CATV brings in the signals of outside stations, the small local audience available to that market's broadcasters is reduced (the so-called *distraction effect*), thereby jeopardizing the local broadcasters' advertising revenue. Thus, while CATV is a response to the consumers' desire to receive all three networks, it has at the same time been viewed as a competitive threat to the survival of small broadcasters and therefore to the government's design for a national television grid of local stations. Furthermore, the FCC fears that, if the local broadcaster is forced to go off the air, only CATV subscribers will be able to receive television signals.

Because of the high cost involved in providing CATV service, (the cable alone cost upwards of $5,000 a mile), it would be provided only in the more populated areas. Thus in the absence of a local broadcasting station, televison service would not be available to the dispersed rural population.

Acting on these fears, in the absence of even one station failure, the FCC extended its authority to regulate all CATV systems. This involved a radical interpretation of Federal authority, which has since been sustained by the Supreme Court. The radical nature of this policy stems from the fact that nearly all CATV systems operate within the state and do not use spectrum space, a national resource. As a result, they lay beyond the conventional definition of Federal authority.

After following this convoluted evolution of public policy, it may be hard to believe but the FCC abandoned its original objective of protecting the small, local broadcaster. When, in 1966, the FCC issued its rules and regulations for CATV, it revealed that it had all but abandoned the idea of protecting television broadcasters in the small towns from CATV competition. Instead, it forbade the entry of CATV systems only into the top 100 markets. Why? Because the big cities were the only place where investors could realistically be expected to build UHF stations, and the FCC feared that the presence of CATV in the big cities might discourage future UHF investors. Thus, CATV systems were permitted to proliferate in the small towns, where they posed their greatest economic threat to the development of local stations, but they were prohibited from entering the big cities, where their economic impact on very large urban broadcasters would have been relatively inconsequential.

In 1972, the FCC altered its objectives again. While making extensive demands on future CATV systems it relaxed its rules to permit CATV to enter the major markets. In doing so, the FCC now argued that CATV would aid in the development of UHF stations (by improving the signals delivered into the home) and that the new, more complex regulations were required to encourage program production. How this would encourage program production was never explained. The essential fact, however, is that bureaucracy and government regulation were expanded.

The Resulting Waste

With more than half of the nation's available television broadcasting capacity lying idle in the UHF band, a significant part of the spectrum space is being wasted. This is a valuable national resource for which there is considerable demand from other types of users. Part of this problem is inherent in the nature of television communications. It consumes a large piece of the spectrum. A single television signal occupies enough spectrum space for 1,200 simultaneous telephone conversations, and 82 such channels have been earmarked for television throughout the nation.

A major contender for part of the spectrum space allocated to television is the private two-way radio service. This service is used for communication by police and fire departments; for dispatching maintenance crews in the power, gas, rail, highway, and other utility industries; for the remote control of machinery and industrial processes; for paging of personnel in an industrial establishment; and for doctors or other professionals when they are away from their offices. The expansion of these services would increase efficiency and reduce costs in broad sections of the economy. There is a body of opinion that holds that these services cannot expand effectively in the spectrum space presently allocated to them. This problem is reported to be especially acute in large cities, where both private radio services and new UHF stations have their greatest potential.

While it helps to reduce the cost of small business, private two-way radio is not itself a small business. Investment in private communication equipment now approaches $1.5 billion. By comparison, the investment in all tangible TV broadcasting property in the United States, at original cost, totals $1.4 billion and its depreciated value, by 1973, was less then half that sum or only $620 million.

Pressure for reconsideration of existing spectrum allocation has been mounting. There are today over 7 million authorized two-way radio systems and the number is increasing at about 10 percent per year. A reallocation of a small part of the spectrum space could provide the private radio services with considerable room for expansion. With this expansion there is likely to occur a decline in equipment costs as a result of production economies, with the result that private two-way radio communication could become a common piece of equipment not only in business, but also in the automobile and in the home.

Errors in Social Engineering

Aside from the distortions resulting from the attempt to impose local service on the television medium, is more local service in fact desirable? Isn't local service more than adequately handled by the radio and newspaper media? As a matter of fact, the degree of localism in news reporting is nowhere as developed as in the United States. Ben Bagdikian, in his book, *The Information Machines*, points out that in Russia, metropolitan Moscow has less than 3 percent of that nation's population but its dailies account for 87 percent of all Russian newspaper circulation. The same is true of Japan where Tokyo-based newspapers account for 70 percent of that nation's newspaper circulation. London dailies also account for 70 percent of that nation's newspaper circulation. But the daily circulation of New York City and Washington, D.C., newspapers *combined* accounts for less than 10 percent of the national total.[7]

In effect there is no national daily in the U.S. The American system has always been geared to local news and local advertising. Perhaps too much so. Consequently, when television, an entirely new medium, made its appearance, it should have been employed as a window on the world rather than merely another means of providing local service. The advent of domestic space satellites in 1974 provides an added dimension to this aspect of video communications, but the present video system of hundreds of small broadcasting stations has made this difficult. Ground distribution of satellite signals is made considerably more complex and expensive than it would have been if the nation's television grid had consisted of broad regional markets.

To implement the objective of local service, the FCC did more than just design a highly atomized system, it also makes it a point of consideration at license renewal time. Every three years the FCC requires that each station draw from its program logs seven randomly selected days of programming from among the three preceding years to constitute a representative week's programming. The second by second account of what was broadcast on each of these seven days is sent to Washington. There are 350 to 400 entries in each day, and reports are obtained from about 2,500 stations (radio and television) for review each year. The result is over 7 million entries. The Renewal Branch of the FCC employs only four people. The task of evaluation is hopelessly lost in minutiae, and the information, even if computerized, is too lacking in meaning to be of any value. The principal objective of these reports, however, is to determine the extent to which the broadcaster was faithful to the government's desire that the broadcaster provide local service.

In an article in the May 1970 issue of the *Industrial and Commercial Law Review,* Kenneth Cox, a former FCC Commissioner, claims that the FCC has all but abandoned its former requirement of local live programming, and for years has not evaluated much of the data collected in the license renewal forms. It is now just a ritual. Nevertheless, the information still piles up in Washington.

The concept of local video service was not only poorly conceived, it was subverted by the FCC itself when the Commission permitted the evolution of the present television networks. The networks created a coordinated nationwide system of programming that achieved by means of the network affiliation contract what the FCC had opposed in its assignment of spectrum space—a wise oversight.

The experiences of the FCC in the broadcasting field raise serious questions regarding the wisdom of having the government plan the structure of an industry. As will be discussed later, this lesson was not lost on the Commissioners when the domestic satellite industry came to them for authorization. In 1973, they opened the field to all comers over the strenuous objections of the FCC staff who preferred a regulated monopoly like AT&T. One of the first effects of this new policy was a 60 percent drop in AT&T's charges for interconnecting television stations. This is another example of the benefits of the process of creative destruction, discussed earlier, where even the nation's largest corporation, until now protected by government regulation, had to bow to the pending entry of new firms and new technology. The industrial planning employed by the government in the field of mass communication was poorly conceived and in large part, is unnecessary.

VI

The Professionals

Intelligence: Public and Private

The United States government spends approximately $5 billion a year and employs over 200,000 persons just to gather information from abroad for its own "private" use.[1] This does not include the State Department, whose ambassadors and technical specialists gather information in nearly every country in the world. In contrast to the government's staggering investment in information, the American public relies on not more than 600 full-time American correspondents assigned abroad by all the mass media and a supporting staff of about 700 foreign nationals.

In effect, the entire nation of over 200 million people depends on this relatively small corps of foreign correspondents for knowledge of events abroad and as a check on its own government's activities in matters of foreign policy and national defense.

Although a great deal of the information gathered by the government in no way bears on national security, it is rarely made available to the public. This information, collected at the public's expense, requires the effort of skilled journalists to ferret it out. The power attributed to the media and to journalists is, in fact, lodged in the quality and credibility of the information that they may (or may not) provide.

There have been a number of opportunities in recent years by which to evaluate the relative abilities of the public and the private intelligence gathering systems.

The Bay of Pigs fiasco, the daring raid that failed to find American prisoners in the Sontay prison camp in North Vietnam, the faulty information preparatory to the incursion into Laos, as well as the generally inferior quality of information obtained by the government regarding conditions in Eastern Europe, Southeast Asia and China, and the failure to accurately assess Soviet and Arab intentions toward Israel in 1973, give testimony to the poor return on its immense investment in information. By comparison, the general public has been much better served (and at much less cost) by its system of mass communications. This is probably best illustrated by the last decade's reporting of the Vietnam War.

In the first half of the 1960s there was little, if any, on-the-spot coverage of Vietnam by the American media. During this period the media merely transmitted to the public the government's press releases. As conduits for government views, the American media helped to paint the administration into a corner with its own rhetoric.

When the American commitment became substantial the media set up shop in Vietnam. The ABC television and radio network employed, in Vietnam, 30 staffers including correspondents, soundmen, editors and producers, and spent upwards of $1 million a year on Vietnam coverage. NBC's staff in Vietnam numbered 25 to 30 and it spent about $2 million a year to obtain about 120 hours of regular programs and 15 hours of specials. The CBS staff in Vietnam numbered about 45 and its costs probably equalled that of NBC. Thus, the three major television and radio networks alone had a staff of over 100 gathering and processing the news in Vietnam.[2]

In addition to the networks, and the equally substantial commitment of the wire services, there was coverage by individual newspapers and broadcast stations. The cost of sending a correspondent on a month's tour of Vietnam came to about $5,000. In the years following 1967 there were generally about 25 correspondents from American media other than the main network and wire news organizations scouring Vietnam for soldiers from back home for personalized interviews.

Through close-ups of what Vietnam was like on the operational level, including the status of the pacification programs, the treatment of civilians, and the morale of the troops, the public began to understand the nature of this unusual decade of military commitment. The improved coverage of the Vietnam War gave rise to doubts regarding the Defense Department's assumptions, predictions, and general competence. This coverage, however, developed late. An earlier start might have helped to reduce the government's sequence of blunders.

It was not easy going all the way. Correspondents frequently reported that the military lied to them. As a more diplomatic reporter expressed it, he had found people in the U.S. Mission and among the military "who saw a higher value than the truth." The official news briefings were widely referred to as the "5 o'clock follies" since the official information officers conducted themselves as if they were public relations men pushing a product, in this case, the war, and wanted to put it in the best light possible.

Fortunately for all concerned, the military rarely employed outright censorship. Thus, the media eventually helped to correct the nation's and the government's view of reality and in the process helped to divert the government from its unproductive course. This culminated in President Johnson's refusal or perhaps inability to stand for renomination for a second term. A poll taken in 1967 by Louis Harris showed that only 18 percent of the public thought that President Johnson was "frank and straightforward" regarding the Vietnam War. By comparison Nixon's credibility factor regarding Vietnam was 43 percent. There probably has never been a more dramatic illustration of the importance of the mass media than its ability to bring to the American people a relatively accurate picture of the situation in Vietnam despite the efforts of the American government to the contrary.

By comparison, in France, where the government indirectly controls the media through strict censorship of news sources, people were far less aware of their own government's activities in Vietnam in the 1950s or in Algeria during that equally painful conflict. Indeed, their media did not even inform them of the Paris student riots of 1971.

The Pentagon Papers

The extraordinary and possibly unprecedented use of subterfuge by President Johnson and his associates may explain the failure of the nation's media to alert the general public and Congress to the nature of the Vietnam affair when it was in its formative stages. The subsequent attitude of the media toward the Government is a subject deserving of study in itself. For the media then adopted a skeptical and ultimately hostile attitude, even when it was not warranted, though this was infrequent. As an example, the media paid little attention to the fact that North Vietnamese troops were in

Cambodia and Laos, and instead blamed America for expansion of the war.

The turning point of the government versus the media aspect of the Vietnam War was the attempt of the Nixon administration to prevent publication of an historical analysis of America's Vietnam policy that had fallen into the hands of the media in April 1971. The Pentagon's 47-volume history of America's involvement in Indochina was extraordinary in its revelation of government ineptitude and fraternal groupthink. There was none of the exposure of military secrets which the government alleged would occur. The public and the professional journalist again found that the government, though headed by a new president and a different political party, nevertheless was intent on protecting the boys in the backroom from public exposure.

The salutary effect of the controversy over publication of the Pentagon Papers was the Supreme Court ruling. In an age in which the chief executive alone can commit the nation to costly and often irreversible policies, early public scrutiny of the assumptions underlying government policies has become an essential part of the democratic process. This can be assured only through the free flow of information.

Justice Brennan noted in his concurring opinion that "never before has the United States (government) sought to enjoin a newspaper from publishing information in its possession." Justice Stewart took particular exception to the government's desire to protect itself by classifying its documents. "When everything is classified, then nothing is classified." Justice Black expressed the opinion that "the press was to serve the governed not the governors. The government's power to censor the press was abolished so that the press would remain forever free to censure the government. . . . Paramount among the responsibilities of a free press is the duty to prevent any part of the government from deceiving the people. . . . "

Public knowledge of the number of troops committed to Vietnam (over 500,000); the number of men killed (over 45,000) and wounded (over 250,000); the large number of aircraft lost (over 6,000); the generally high economic price ($2 billion a *month*); the lack of control over the Vietnamese countryside despite the vast commitment reported by the media; the awareness of government deception; and the moral issues raised by the war (especially its effect on the people we were supposedly defending) all led to the public's rejection of the government's Vietnam policy.

Once the facts started to flow, America's media, rather than its democratically-elected government, held the confidence of the people. The effect that this experience will have on the concept of government deserves more attention than it has yet received from scholars, the media, and the government. In time, its implications could be profound, and not only for the American people.

Secretiveness

The task of the professional journalist is clear. He functions as the antagonist of the bureaucracy. His objective, if not his duty, is to make public that which the bureaucracy seeks to keep confidential. Rarely is national security at issue. The secretiveness of government employees is for their own protection rather than for the protection of the nation. Foolishness, waste, and the desire to accumulate and wield power for its own sake, are some of the motives underlying their secretiveness. As an example, the cloak of executive privilege was extended to the following important questions:

1. The Defense Department refused to produce generals to testify before a Congressional committee regarding army surveillance of civilians.
2. The State Department would not discuss its plans or explain its policies as regards foreign economic policy (Congress subsequently voted to discontinue the foreign aid program).
3. The executive branch would not explain to Congress the standards for listing *American* citizens in an internal security computer.

These are examples of information requested by *elected* officials of *appointed* officials which the latter chose to conceal. Yet in startling contrast to the government's secretiveness regarding the domestic and economic policies listed above, the following article appeared in the *New York Times* on October 6, 1971. It was filed by Reuters, a European news service:

FB-111's DEPLOYED WITH NUCLEAR ARMS

Omaha, Oct. 5 (Reuters)—The FB-111 bomber, a descendant of the politically controversial and trouble-plagued TFX, has begun to take over some of the burdens of the United States nuclear deterrent force, the Strategic Air Command disclosed today.

At least 12 of the swing-wing planes are now on constant ground alert at SAC bases in the Northeast.

Each of the supersonic planes is armed with six nuclear bombs with a total yield of about five megatons, equal to the explosive force of five million tons of TNT.

Four of the weapons are nestled in bomb bays and one is mounted on an external rack under each wing.

The bombers are poised on alert pads at Pease Air Force Base at Portsmouth, N.H., and at Plattsburgh Air Force Base in northern New York.

The command acknowledged today that a portion of the FB-111 force had been written into the nation's nuclear war plan, an integrated operations plan for all strategic forces of the United States

and the North Atlantic Treaty Organization. But a spokesman at
SAC headquarters here said he could not disclose the exact number
of FB-111 that had been declared operational.

Isn't this information the "real stuff," the sort that
cloak-and-dagger types risk their lives to get their hands on,
the sort of information that should be classified?

This brief comparison between what the government
reveals and what it conceals illustrates what those who
observe the government at close range have always known—
that American news reporters and not "foreign powers" are
the government's principal adversary. It is from the American
journalist, and therefore the American public, that most
documents are classified. In this the government acknowl-
edges that the real power of the media is not that they can
influence the public but rather that they can inform the
public. The power with which the media are generally
credited is inherent in *what* they communicate. It is the facts
(knowledge), not the media, that possess power. To the
extent that the bureaucrats can keep the facts that underly
their decisions to themselves, their power is enhanced. Con-
versely, to the extent that the public is informed, *their* power
is enhanced.

The contest over the control of information is a contest
over the sum and substance of power. To share information is
to share the essence of power. The effect of the journalistic
function is thus to temper the government's attempts to
make the governed more easily governable. On the other
hand, the extent to which the governed are informed of their
government's activities is the extent to which their freedom is
assured. The conflicts of interest are obvious and they are
inherent in the roles played by the protagonists.

Examples of tension or built-in conflict are many, and
they are increasing of late. In this contest for facts the truth

has been sought regarding the administration's policy on a wide range of issues, including school busing, ecology, arms purchases and arms sales, the surveillance of civilians, consumer protection, Indian affairs, and the energy shortage.

Selling the Pentagon Affair

The journalist's power to inform, however, is not beyond corruptibility, noble though his intent may be. If the journalist or the owners or managers of the media themselves tamper with the information obtained from their investigative activities then their credibility (that is, their "power") is endangered and with it their function as the public's information gathering service.

Several vital issues inadvertently combined over a single television program which focused attention on this problem. It involved the CBS television documentary on the Defense Department's domestic public relations activities, referred to in the preceding chapter. The CBS documentary, *The Selling of the Pentagon*, was broadcast nationwide in the spring of 1971. The program was attacked by the Vice President and by several members of Congress on the grounds that it engaged in unusual distortions. It was charged that the program's producer took words uttered by a Pentagon official in answer to one set of questions and used them as an answer to a different set of questions.

Representative Harley Staggers of the House Commerce Committee subpoenaed CBS's original film from which the program was assembled to investigate these allegations. Dr. Frank Stanton, the President of CBS, refused to produce them on principle, citing the First Amendment on freedom of the press. The Committee found him in contempt, a finding that failed to pass a vote of the full House; at which point this highly celebrated affair disappeared from public view. It was, however, a very significant encounter.

This affair was two-sided. The reaction against the program was in truth motivated by its conclusions—that the Defense Department was spending the taxpayers' hard-earned money to propagandize the same American taxpayers to favor increased arms expenditures. This, indeed, was an activity unbecoming this particular agency of the government. In addition, a number of examples of the Defense Department's public relations techniques shown in this documentary were distasteful. These included a demonstration of how to kill an adversary, performed at a shopping center in Ohio before an audience of children and housewives. The documentary also reported on movies shown to the public in which the Defense Department advocated a particular approach to foreign policy, a public relations activity in which even the State Department does not engage.

These were clearly issues of considerable importance, though unsensational since they were no secret to anyone who took an interest in such matters. The Staggers' committee did not fault the program's conclusions, but sought to impugn them on the grounds that the program's producer engaged in questionable "editing" techniques. On this issue, Staggers was supported by the evidence.

The zealousness of the CBS news team caused their editing to get in the way of their reporting. They did in fact so radically alter the sequence of responses in an interview that their critics were able to shift the public's attention from the program's content to the program's techniques and in the process to challenge the medium's credibility.

Thus, in editing their news tapes CBS presented as a direct six-sentence quotation, a statement from a colonel composed of a first sentence from page 55 of his prepared text, followed by a second statement from page 36, followed by a third and a fourth from page 48, and a fifth from page 73, and a sixth from page 88. When shown on television it appeared that the Colonel's reply was made verbatim as shown.

In the same documentary, a sequence with Daniel Henkin, Assistant Secretary of Defense for Public Affairs, was so manipulated that it affected the meaning of the response. The following is an example of this form of editing. The program as shown on the air contained the following question and reply:

> Roger Mudd (CBS): What about your public displays of military equipment at state fairs and shopping centers? What purpose does that serve?
>
> Mr. Henkin: Well, I think it serves the purpose of informing the public about their armed forces. I believe the American public has the right to request information about the armed forces, to have speakers come before them, to ask questions, and to understand the need for our armed forces, why we ask for the funds that we do ask for, how we spend these funds, what are we doing about such problems as drugs—and we do have a drug problem in the armed forces; what are we doing about the racial problem—and we do have a racial problem. I think the public has a valid right to ask us these questions.

This, on the other hand, is how Mr. Henkin *actually* answered the question:

> Mr. Henkin: Well, I think it serves the purpose of informing the public about their armed forces. It also has the ancillary benefit, I would hope, of simulating interest in recruiting as we move or try to move to zero draft calls and increased reliance on volunteers for our armed forces. I think it is very important that the American youth has an opportunity to learn about the armed forces.

The answer Mr. Henkin was *shown* to be giving had been transposed from his answer to another question a couple of pages along in the transcribed interview. In that sequence, Roger Mudd had asked Mr. Henkin whether the sort of thing he was now talking about—drug problems and racial problems—was "the sort of information that gets passed at state fairs by sergeants who are standing next to rockets." To which Mr. Henkin replied:

> Mr. Henkin: No, I didn't—wouldn't limit that to sergeants standing next to any kind of exhibits. I knew—I thought we were discussing speeches and all.

Here is how the same exchange was edited for network television:

> Mr. Mudd: Well, is that the sort of information about the drug problem you have and racial problem you have and the budget problems you have—is that the sort of information that gets passed out at state fairs by sergeants who are standing next to rockets?
> Mr. Henkin: No, I wouldn't limit that to sergeants standing next to any kind of exhibit. Now, there are those who contend that this is propaganda. I do not agree with this.

The part about discussing "speeches and all" had been omitted; the part about propaganda comes from a few lines above Mr. Henkin's actual answer and was, in fact, a reference to charges that the Pentagon was using talk of the "increasing Soviet threat" as propaganda to influence the size of the military budget.[2]

In the resulting hullabaloo even the First Amendment privileges were unnecessarily exposed to danger when Representative Staggers subpoenaed the program's original materials. This might have become another precedent for limiting the profession's right to privileged information. Staggers knew all along precisely what changes had been made by CBS in its editing. His committee was simply out to penetrate the veil that protects the journalist's sources and the confidentiality of their work materials.

This affair uncovered an extremely important issue. It highlighted the fact that news reporting and advocacy are inherently incompatible. Excessive zeal on the part of reporters in advancing a point of view violates the profession's function. In effect, "advocacy journalism" is a contradiction of terms. Those who advance this school of thought have abandoned concern for the journalist's credibility in favor of their own point of view. It is an arrogance born of the myth that the media are powerful because the audience is malleable. But the public is not weak minded as some believe. Facts are enough to call their attention to the issues. Editorials and news analyses have their place in the media but they should not be blended with the straight news reporting that is the backbone of mass communications. From the public's standpoint there is no difference between those who advocate a point of view out of sincerity and those who are motivated by monetary or psychological considerations. In the end the public is shortchanged in the accuracy or comprehensiveness of the information it receives.

Actors or Critics

So great is the activist urge today that many journalists have even gone beyond advocacy and have become actual participants in the events—in effect, have themselves become news makers.

The power of the media, however, is based not on its technology but on its credibility. The impropriety of reporters, editors, publishers, or media owners participating in the events on which they report is a serious threat to the role of the media as a reliable source of information in the American system.

There is today considerable confusion regarding the proper role and behavior of the professional journalist, editor and media owner. Is it a bribe when a member of the news staff, a news editor, a publisher or a broadcaster accepts gifts, awards, free trips, or tickets to entertainment events? *Editor and Publisher*, a leading trade journal, lists more than 130 prizes for newsmen. The source of many of these "awards" are special interest groups. They offer prizes ranging up to $2,500. The winner of the Pulitzer Prize, by comparison, receives only $1,000.[3] These sums are relatively small, but then so was the value of the vicuna coat accepted by Sherman Adams, President Eisenhower's powerful executive assistant who was drummed out of office after the media disclosed his acceptance of this "token of appreciation" from an industrialist.

Should those serving the public in the field of mass communications be any less scrupulous? Should they become involved in politics? Should they write speeches for political candidates, manage campaigns, advise candidates on the use of media and generally hobnob with politicians or representatives of special interests?

Herbert Klein, the former White House Communications Director, alternated between being editor of the *San Diego Union* and a political activist for Richard Nixon. (He is now vice president of MetroMedia Corporation). Erwin Canham, Editor-in-chief of the highly respected *Christian Science Monitor*, lobbies for revenue sharing and has served as President of the U. S. Chamber of Commerce. Tom Wicker, a columnist and associate editor of the *New York Times*, has made a number of public appearances in which he attacked

American foreign policy, particularly regarding Vietnam. Arnaud de Borchgrave, a senior editor of *Newsweek* assigned to the Middle East, has been active on behalf of Anwar Sadat, president of Egypt.

Can the public rely on the media's objectivity in news reporting when its reporters, editors, publishers and owners unabashedly compromise themselves financially and politically? Unlike political institutions whose public trust is inscribed in the statutes, the media now float in an undefined space that separates commerce and its credo, *caveat emptor*, from the ethically defined professions of law, medicine, and politics.

At some point, and soon, the media professionals, from reporters to owners, will have to decide whether they are participants or observers. To investigate and to report the facts is the duty of the media's professionals. To attempt to lead the public is to take sides, to have a vested interest, in effect, to abandon objectivity for commitment. At that point, the media professional has changed professions: he has become a politician. If this involves an editor or an owner, they have, in effect, converted their medium from a dispassionate and uncommitted source of objective information into a party publication or party broadcast facility. In truth it cannot be played both ways.

A Profile

Who are the professional journalists? What kind of people are they? Is there any substance to the romantic figure drawn by American fiction?

A survey of foreign correspondents published by Leo Bogart reported that the typical foreign correspondent is a married male in his forties; a college graduate with over ten years' experience in journalism, and not less than three years in his foreign post. His closest friends include local foreign nationals whose newspapers he reads regularly and whose language he is able to speak fluently (except for those in Asia).

Nearly half of those responding to Bogart's survey reported that they considered themselves political "liberals," 38 percent thought of themselves as moderates and 10 percent as conservatives. Nearly 60 percent identified with the Democratic party, 21 percent with the Republican and 15 percent as independents.[4]

The old "Front Page" image of the young free-lance high school dropout whose style was more swashbuckle than academic, who was more detective than researcher, is a myth. Fewer than 4 percent of all correspondents serving the American media abroad did not attend college. Three-quarters of the foreign correspondents are college graduates; a third of these attended graduate school. About 94 percent of all foreign correspondents are accompanied by their wives and children.

In fact, the foreign correspondent serving the American public is an educated and seasoned professional who is steeped in the knowledge of the environment to which he is assigned. He is also well paid.

Domestic Journalism

At home, the nation's capital is the prestige news center. The resident press corps in Washington numbers approximately 650 full-time professionals, slightly more than the number of foreign correspondents serving American mass media abroad.

Hopefully, what they produce is a balanced account of the government's views, relevant facts that they are able to assemble, and the views of the opposition. The information sent home by the members of the Washington press corps, however, is subject to assault by a veritable army of publicly financed full-time government public information specialists—at the last count numbering 5,200 in the Executive Branch alone.

During the Nixon administration, the President's Office of Information has, to some extent, drawn upon this immense resource to make an end-run around the Washington press corps by sending copies of speeches and press releases directly to local newspapers and broadcasting stations.

In addition to the press corps, approximately thirteen radio and television broadcast groups have special news bureaus in Washington, D.C. The average capital news bureau files 60 to 100 items a week. None of these news bureaus cover the basic news events nor the White House since the radio and television networks and the wire services perform this function. The news bureaus focus on Capitol Hill and provide their local audiences with special angles and coverage of important but less conspicuous issues of interest to a specific locality.

Medium sized news bureaus in the capital, such as that of Time, Inc., Cox Broadcasting, or Storer Broadcasting, cost about $300,000 a year to operate. Apart from the networks, the largest Washington news bureau in the broadcasting field belongs to Westinghouse. Its operating expenses, including salaries, approach $1 million a year.

The "stars" of journalism, however, are neither the foreign correspondents nor those assigned to the nation's capital, prestigious as they may be, but rather the columnists and pundits.

The television pundits like Eric Sevaried, David Brinkley,

and Howard K. Smith are the highest paid of their profession, and earn considerably more than newpaper columnists. But newspaper columnists are generally better paid than news editors. Art Buchwald was recently reported to be the nation's highest-paid columnist, with earnings of $125,000 a year from his column, and another $50,000 from lecturing.

Clearly such news columns generate large incomes for their syndicates. Jack Anderson's *Washington Merry-Go-Round* annually grosses about $300,000 for its syndicate. Most successful columns bring in about $200,000 a year. Generally, the syndicators split the column's income 50-50 with the columnists, who must pay their own expenses. But columnists have to write three articles a week, which allows little time for thought or research. The consequence is that the columnist displaces newspaper space that might be put to better use, particularly news reporting. The problem, however, is that syndicated columnists are relatively inexpensive, while reportage is expensive (and dangerous).

For example, a small newspaper may pay as little as $10 a week for Art Buchwald's column, since the syndicate salesman either sells cheap or not at all. The top prices paid for columns in larger cities, where there is some newspaper competition, run as high as $225 a week. More typically, in most large cities columns are available for about $50 a week. This is much less than the lowest weekly salary ($300) paid a reporter on the larger dailies.[5]

The economics of the situation clearly indicate that newspaper columnists and television and radio pundits will be an important part of the media scene for some time. Indeed, it is surprising that there are so few, considering the relative costs involved. Unfortunately, few of the columnists and pundits have carried on the tradition of investigative reporting which

Drew Pearson made his hallmark. But, as Jack Anderson, his successor, can testify, investigative reporting can be very risky. It is generally safer to be clever or passionate about current events.

VII

The Underground

Television and the Youth Rebellion

Probably no group in our society is more likely to reflect the influence of television than today's younger generation. Remember that today's average young adult has spent approximately four thousand hours in front of the video screen even before his first day of school.[1] If television exerts a deep influence on people, the values and behavior of the young should in some way reflect the impact of this tremendous exposure. What, in fact, has been the nature of their experience and their behavior?

One of the more noticeable characteristics of children's programs is that they carry twice the number of commercials as do adult programs (16 per hour). Television thus makes the American child a premature participant in our consumer society. By circumventing the natural barrier of illiteracy among the two to six year age group through the visual appeal of its images, television has succeeded in introducing children very early to products and even brands which would not otherwise come to their attention.

Observers of this phenomenon emphasize the ease with which children's appetites are thus stimulated and at the same time the equal ease with which they have been conditioned to expect their desires to be satisfied. Most mothers are pleased to respond to what seems to them a simple enough preference on the part of the child for an item that would be purchased in any event. A survey of 1,500 mothers undertaken by the ABC Television Network revealed that 65 percent of the mothers take their children with them when they go to the supermarket. In the majority of cases, children influenced the mother in the selection of cereals, soft drinks, snacks, toothpaste, and soups. It was also estimated that, on the average, $1.66 more was spent each week for products specifically requested by children. Based on approximately 18 million households with children this adds up to over $1 billion a year of *additional* spending by parents as a result of their children's influence.[2]

Because of his purported responsiveness to suggestion and his influence at home, the pre-teen viewer is an important member of the television audience. By the age of two, children are counted in the audience ratings. And children between the ages of two and eleven make up nearly 23 percent of the viewing population.[3]

Suprisingly, the younger generation has not matured into a generation of avaricious fiends. Indeed, the very opposite has occurred. The principal characteristic of the first generation of young adults who grew up with television has been their rejection of "materialism" and the life style that it engenders. Either their early experience as consumers immunized them to the pleasures of pursuing possessions or television's influence was transitory and more powerful cultural forces were at work.

An unexpected product of their early and intense exposure to mass media is their extraordinary understanding of mass communications. *En masse* the youth of this period revealed an astonishing knowledge of the technical and psychological aspects of this complex subject. They knew for example, that to call attention to their ideas, which were in opposition to a broad range of political and social policies and institutions, they would have to antagonize and at the same time, win over, the older generation. Thus, intuitively, without a central plan, America's youth coalesced into an amorphous "movement" and created a counterculture that challenged the superficial customs and mores a society holds more sacred (without fully realizing it) than their gods. At the same time they created several nationwide news services that linked together a formidable underground newspaper system—with no one planning, directing, financing, or even calling for their creation. And as we shall see, they were successful in almost every one of their objectives, even to the point of winning over the older generation to their counter-cultural innovations which were intended simply as the irri-tant that called attention to their social and political program.

A by-product of the youth rebellion has been the lessons that it taught regarding the state of mass communication in the United States. They faced no serious legal or economic barriers in their media enterprises, evidence that there is free entry in this field. More important, considering the views to which their media gave expression, they showed that there is still much to be said for the American reputation for political freedom.

The Movement and Its Media

The growth of the underground press from its inception in 1964, is amazing. In his book, *The Underground Press*, Robert J. Glessing lists by name over 450 different underground newspapers published in nearly every city in the United States. He estimates their combined circulation at about 5 million. When multiple readers of each copy are considered, a total audience of about 10 million is probably a conservative estimate of the "reach" of the underground press.[4] Considering that there are 20 million high school and college students in the United States this represents a substantial part of American youth. In addition to newspapers this audience is served by several hundred college radio stations which reach millions of young people on and off campus. Many commercial radio stations also appeal to their taste and several magazines such as *Ramparts* and *Avant Garde* were part of the "underground" system.

The devotion of this audience to its media is evident from the fact that these media have drawn hundreds of thousands of young people from great distances to events ranging from rock music concerts to political demonstrations.

These "underground" media are underground in spirit rather than in response to any real need for secrecy. Thus, despite the fact that some of the underground newspapers have published details on how to make Molotov cocktails, how to make false claims for "lost" travelers checks, how to charge another person's telephone for long distance calls (in 1970 AT&T reported $22 million worth of "free" calls, in 1965 the total was less than $3 million), almost no one has been sent to jail. Nearly all of the underground newspapers in the United States are sent through the mail, hawked on street corners and are available in shops catering to young people and students. There is, in fact, not the slightest resemblance between the American "movement" and its "underground" media and the *samizdat* papers circulating today in the U.S.S.R.—or between the treatment accorded those involved in these activities here and that in the U.S.S.R..

True, some of these publications have, on occasion, been

harassed by local authorities. (Sometimes for good reason, as when the now defunct *Washington Free Press* pictured a local magistrate masturbating with the subtitle "He Comm D'Judge.") Usually this harassment is uncalled for, as when underground papers are indicted for obscenity in cities where "adult bookstores" are permitted to operate; or when youthful street vendors receive tickets for jaywalking when stepping off the curb to sell their newspapers; or when printers are induced not to service them. In New Orleans, harassment had gone to such lengths that one underground newspaper won a Federal restraining order enjoining the city and state police from harassing the newspaper's vendors. The overall effect of this harassment, however, has not been repressive. These publications have increased in number and in circulation. They cease publication only when the editors or their readers lose interest, and new publications are continually taking the place of the old.

The "alternative" character of the underground press is expressed by the type of news it prints and the nature of its interpretation. The issues that are the focus of attention in the underground media are subject to change but while they are being pursued they constitute the "causes" on which the media and the movement base their reason for being. Opposition to the Vietnam War had been one of the movement's principal causes, although the underground media originated in the enigmatic free speech movement that flared briefly in the west coast at UCLA in the early sixties. On the east coast, disarmament served as the focus of the SDS in its early days. Both of these groups emerged suddenly just before the height of American involvement in Vietnam, and later dissolved into the amorphous, all encompassing "movement." With the Vietnam war over, with abortion sanctioned by the Supreme Court, and with military conscription at an end, the future of the "movement" and of its media is in doubt. These were their major causes up until 1973. Whether being anti-establishment runs deeper than these issues remains to be seen.

The underground media however, were a phenomenon of some importance and warrant closer scrutiny, particularly when considering such issues as media influence and media control.

Those underground media with the largest circulation were the ones with the greatest preoccupation with sex. Thus, the *Village Voice* (120,000), *Los Angeles Free Press* (95,000), *Berkeley Barb* (85,000), and *East Village Other* (65,000) carried extensive classified ads devoted to sexual matters. The big underground papers on the west coast had a greater preoccupation with sexual deviation than those in other parts of the country.

The underground newspapers with a substantially smaller circulation, such as the *D.C. Gazette* (5,000); *Quick—Silver Times* (20,000); *Harry* (12,000); *Off Our Backs* (5,000); carried very few, if any, sex ads.

There was also a "class" distinction among some of the underground newspapers. The *Berkeley Barb* (now defunct) was essentially an underground tabloid. In one edition, eight of its twenty pages were devoted to sex ads. The balance of the paper consisted of sex related articles and very brief pieces on standard underground themes. Its west coast competitor, the *Los Angeles Free Press*, on the other hand, conveyed the tone of underground establishment. Its format was more conventional and its articles were longer, better written and covered a wider range of subjects than the *Barb*. A similar relationship is evident among the big underground newspapers on the east coast where the *Village Voice* is underground establishment catering to the liberal intellectuals and the *East Village Other* plays the role of the tabloid, catering to underground anti-intellectuals.

The Underground News Collectives

The high degree of uniformity amid the diversity that typifies the underground press is attributable to the presence of underground news services. There are four major coordinating news services—Liberation News Service (LNS), Underground Press Syndicate (UPS), Cooperative High School Independent Press Service (CHIPS), and College Press Service (CPS)—that act as an interchange among the hundreds of underground media. They also provide original material, much of which finds its way into the otherwise independent local underground outlets.

The Underground Press Syndicate and the Liberation News Service are the major news services of the general underground press. CHIPS and CPS perform the same function for the underground high school and college press, respectively. Both in their tone and in their objectives, LNS and UPS differ markedly.

Liberation News Service (LNS) operates out of a large basement with an offset printing press located one block from the Columbia University campus in New York City. It obtains its principal financial backing from donations. A major donor in the past was the Joint Council of Churches.

A "collective" of eight young men and women run the service. Three coordinating editors, appointed from the collective every two weeks on a rotating basis, manage the writing and selection of articles for biweekly ten-page "packets" sent to a mailing list which, it is claimed, numbers 600 subscribers, including most of the underground newspapers.

The biweekly packets which LNS distributes lack the vitriolic tone, adolescent vocabulary, and four-letter words that typify the underground media they service. The articles are generally well written, reproduced by photo-offset from typed manuscript and printed on large 11 x 16 inch sheets.

The thrust of the material is political with the focus on anti-war issues, racial and economic injustices, and feminist themes. If at all possible, the injustices are linked in one way or another to U.S. policies, domestic or foreign. The members of the collective who were interviewed by the author viewed the United States as the "enemy of the world" and expressed strong sympathy for the socialist and communist systems. Basically, however, they are radicals rather than revolutionaries, since they look to education and evolution as the means of achieving the universal collectivization which they admire.

The bias of this news service (and the underground press in general) is apparent from what they choose *not* to report. The LNS did not report on the invasion of Czechoslavakia or the subsequent repression in that country. LNS has also ignored the Russian repression of Soviet intellectuals and the considerable *underground* literature there. The service did not carry a single article on the Soviet show trials of Jews, their cultural repression by Soviet authorities, or the protests in the U.S. and Russia regarding Soviet treatment of Jews.

In domestic matters, problems of welfare do not attract the attention of LNS (or the underground in general) nor do the problems of the sociology of poverty or the education of the poor. The LNS packets and the underground media, in general, focus on identifying and reporting sources of discontent, rather than their solution.

The *Underground Press Syndicate* (UPS) is the other major news service serving the general underground media. It provides a free bi-weekly packet to 200 underground newspapers. It is operated by three women, 22 to 25 years old, one of whom is a college graduate. As at LNS, all are white.

UPS operates from a loft in the Union Square section of Manhattan.

The UPS editors are devoted principally to the cause of feminism. Indeed, they see this issue as taking precedence over all other issues. In political matters they favor collectivism. However, unlike LNS's affection for socialism, UPS representatives favor no government at all. Their millennium is anarchy.

In style and content, UPS differs markedly from LNS. UPS employs the vitriol and four-letter words that typify their subscribers' writing styles. Their articles are brief, nasty, and generally lacking in substance.

The UPS loft serves as a residence for its editors who, like the LNS group, draw small sums for their own support. The UPS obtains its principal financial backing from the Bell & Howell Corporation. This is facilitated through an arrangement whereby UPS collects copies of all underground newspapers for microfilming by Bell & Howell, who then sells the microfilm to libraries and splits the fees 50-50 with UPS.

UPS also operates the Free Ranger Advertising Coop which serves as an advertising representative for over 100 underground newspapers. It claims a combined *readership* (as distinct from circulation) of 6 million. The UPS claims to have obtained over $200,000 in national ad revenues for the underground media in the 1968-1971 period. This was an addition to the ad revenues obtained by underground newspapers locally.

How To Start a High School Underground

In a booklet by this title Cooperative High School Independent Press Service (CHIPS) introduces the high school reader to the spirit of the movement:

Some (students) are dropping out of school, others are burning down their schools, and many are starting underground papers. While all three of these things are quite commendable, this booklet is only about the last one—starting an independent paper at a public high school.

After a competent description of methods to be used in staffing and printing the paper, the booklet advocates distribution of the underground newspaper on the school's grounds rather than in the school's general area. This is designed as the staff's first confrontation with authority and a step in its radicalization.

The (school) administration knows that if the paper is underground, they have absolutely no control over it, and that scares them. So they set up little "conditions" for approval, hoping to at least be able to exercise some control over it. Of course you will have to consider local circumstances. In general I would suggest that you tell the school board to take their compromise and shove it up their ass. You shouldn't have to compromise your rights.

As its principal service this High School Press Syndicate distributes a biweekly packet consisting of 16 pages of mimeographed news and commentary for which their 60 subscribing publications pay $4.00 a year.

The following are the titles of some of the news articles contained in this packet. The articles are intended for reproduction by subscribing high school newspapers:

Bugs Pop Up Everywhere
Army Files on High School Students Uncovered
Principal Rips Off Angela
Teachers Suspended for "Disorderly Conduct"
Mayday: A Brief Listing of Events
Students Force Resignation of Principal
Sex Discrimination Opposed In Little League

Principal Attacked for Racial Work
Teacher Dismissed As Being Witch
Principal Fined For Hair Expulsion
FBI Files Reveal Wide Range of Groups Being Spied On.

One "CHIPS" news packet carried an article that began:

The Student Information Center is in the process of putting together a pamphlet on birth control and abortion for *high school aged women.*

In another article in the same issue an upstate New York youngster solicited for "ideas on underground activities" in which he included an example:

Wanted: different methods of destruction against society if retaliation is needed, such as starting thousands of fires during the dry season in wooded sections.

The coordinating group at the next level of education is the *College Press Service*. It has an audience consisting of about 300 college newspapers most of which are not part of the underground establishment but are newspapers supported by college funds. In addition, about 20 conventional underground newspapers subscribe to this service. At last report, the CPS editorial staff consisted of four persons in a Washington, D.C., office and a few correspondents located in different cities and campuses. Three correspondents were reported to be abroad, one each in Paris, Saigon and Beirut.

The CPS performs the same basic exchange and editorial functions for the college media as CHIPS does for the high school media. CPS, however, distributes its eight-page packets twice a week and charges, but doesn't always collect, between $50 and $450 a year for the service. Its materials are not mimeographed, as is CHIPS's but are printed on its own offset equipment.

In spirit and tone the CPS material is more restrained and thoughtful than its high school counterpart. Its articles generally are lengthy discussions of significant issues.

Included in one packet was a long exposé on classified research at UCLA, written by Daniel Dennett, an associate professor of philosophy at the university. CPS also informed its subscribing newspapers how to charge someone else's telephone when making long distance calls, and provided a feminist attack on the male sexual ego.

The Cost of Entering the Underground

The underground media taught an important lesson about freedom of entry in the field of mass communications. A newspaper of relatively modest circulation (less than 100,000) can be published at very nominal cost. This is made possible by the photo-offset process which involves the "photographing" of typed pages, pictures, and sketches. The newspaper can be prepared for the printer simply by pasting typed text and photographs on an ordinary sheet of paper. The cost of a photo-offset newspaper averages approximately one dollar per page for every 250 copies. Thus, a run of 10,000 copies of an eight-page edition would cost less than $350, plus a nominal charge for machine folding of the newspaper. Color printing adds to this cost.

This investment can generate a gross revenue of $1,000 to $2,500 for newspapers selling at 10¢ to 25¢ a copy. This income is generally split with the vendor. Advertising by local boutiques, record companies, movie theatres, abortion clinics, water bed salesmen, and bookstores brings in additional revenue.

Since the staff, consisting of a handful of students or

recent graduates, generally work without pay or for pocket money, labor is also a modest expense. However, there is almost always a deficit since not all copies are sold, and there are overhead expenses such as rent, heat, electricity, telephone, postage, and supplies. Nevertheless, the underground press has shown that the economic requirements for publishing a newspaper need not be a matter of real concern for those intent on communicating their point of view.

With a relatively modest investment totaling about $2,000 it is possible to purchase equipment such as an IBM selectric typewriter with a number of interchangeable typefaces, a headline machine which produces large bold type, and art equipment—which together with the photo-offset process can render a professional looking product.

Some of the underground newspapers are distributed free of charge (as are many establishment weeklies). They rely on advertising or local donations. Similarly, some of the smaller underground newspapers do not charge for classified ads. The inability of most of the underground newspapers to guarantee a minimum circulation or even to be certain of a regular publication schedule precludes them from attracting national or regional advertising revenue on a major scale. In several instances where these requirements were met, the underground newspaper became a successful economic operation.

Of the 79 newspapers subscribing to the Underground Press Syndicate in 1968 (increased to 130 in 1971) 28% reported that they were profitable. The other 72% were breaking even or losing money. The Glessing study reported that the *Berkeley Barb*, owned by Max Scherr, had a profit of $265,000 in 1969. A large part of this profit, however, was due to a salary scale in which staffers received $1.65 per hour and the editors received "nominal weekly wages." When the fact that the owner was earning $5,000 a week became known, most of the staff resigned. That this degree of exploitation of "turned-on" youth was possible must say something about their credulity.

Testing the Establishment

By pressing up against the bounds of convention the underground media and the youth culture have subjected the First Amendment to considerable pressure. (Where the government has the power to censure, as in the field of broadcasting, there is evidence as described below that by 1971 this pressure had begun to succeed in weakening the will to protect the freedom of the press.) Thus, the *Los Angeles Free Press*, which has an audited circulation of 95,000, one of the largest weeklies in the nation, was indicted after it published the names of state undercover narcotics agents in California. The list, including home addresses and telephone numbers, appeared under the headline, "There Should Be No Secret Police." The names of the undercover agents had been obtained from a former mail clerk in the state attorney general's office.

Publication of the roster was not in itself illegal. But, after a long deliberation, the jury convicted the newspaper for being a "fence" under the stolen goods statute. The editors could have received a sentence of up to 19 years in prison. The State Supreme Court in 1973 reversed the lower court's decision on the grounds that the editors did not know that the information was "stolen."

The implications of the lower court's decision for the establishment press were far reaching, and received the immediate attention of a three column analysis in the *Wall Street Journal*.[5] Said the article: "If this decision is not overturned by a higher court [it will force the establishment press to] limit its sources of information, censor itself and be more hesitant in exposing government malfeasance."

Just a year earlier, another court, faced with precisely the same type of situation, drew a different conclusion. Senator Thomas Dodd lost a similar case involving columnist Drew Pearson, who published documents stolen from the Senator's files. In the *Free Press* case, however, the defendant was not a powerful member of the establishment, but a medium continually at odds with the authorities.

The Drug Lyric Affair

The underground media involved broadcasting as well as newspapers. Here too the basic freedoms were tested.

As is its custom every Wednesday, the seven members of the Federal Communications Commission met in their private chambers on February 24, 1971, to deliberate on matters brought before it by the FCC staff. Several months earlier the Department of the Army had made a presentation to the Commission regarding its concern over the broadcasting of songs that tend to glorify the use of drugs. The Commission now voted, five in favor, one opposed, and one abstaining, to release a public notice that "relates to a subject of current and pressing concern: the use of language [lyrics] tending to promote or glorify the use of illegal drugs. . . . The licensees [of broadcasting stations] must make the judgement and cannot properly follow a policy of playing such records without someone in a responsible position knowing the content of the lyrics. . . . Such a pattern of operation. . *raises serious questions as to whether continued operation of the station is in the public interest*. In short, we expect broadcast licensees to ascertain, before broadcast, the lyrics or words of recorded musical or spoken selections played on their stations."[6]

The implications of this public notice are profound: first, for its origin, a presentation made by the U.S. Army[7]; second, for its threat to revoke a broadcast license when the Commissions's (or the military's) judgment on broadcast content was not adhered to, and third, it reveals how uninformed the government was regarding the scope and development of the underground press, whose influence among youth exceeded by far that of radio stations.

This challenge made strange bedfellows. Almost immediately a number of major broadcast groups including RKO General, a subsidiary of General Tire which is a major defense contractor, and Pacifica Foundation, a radical noncommercial broadcast group, filed a joint appeal with the FCC for reconsideration of this policy.

As a result, the FCC tempered its public notices to suggest that it was merely highlighting an already inherent part of licensee obligation. But the public notice was not withdrawn, and the government's position that it could exercise its authority over program content was advanced another step.

In the one dissenting opinion, Commissioner Nicholas Johnson noted that "drug abuse *is* a serious problem (but) not merely among the young." The commissioner's dissent called attention to songs that glorify the use of alcohol and that there are more alcoholics in one city, San Francisco, than there are narcotics addicts in the entire nation.

Commissioner Johnson concluded that the other commissioners were really joining in an attempt to repress the youth culture. He saw this as a "thinly veiled political move." To illustrate his point, Johnson revealed that many of the song lyrics singled out as objectionable by the army were not related to drugs but rather to social commentary, such as:

Itemize the things you covet
As you squander through your life
Bigger cars, bigger houses
Term insurance for your wife.

Investigating College Radio

Three weeks after issuing the order regarding drug lyrics the FCC launched a comprehensive investigation of college radio stations.

Of the more than 2,300 institutions of higher education in the United States, nearly half have their own radio stations. These stations include high-powered facilities that broadcast to the local community, low-powered stations (10 watts or less) whose signals are confined to the local campus, and a strange breed called the *carrier current* facility. The first two types operate under noncommercial licenses regulated by the Federal Communications Commission. As licensees, they are subject to the rules of the FCC. But the third type of facility, the unlicensed carrier current service, has not been significantly controlled by the FCC.

Approximately 450 colleges and universities operate *unlicensed* radio facilities in the carrier current radio service. The radio signals used in this service are conducted along the electric power distribution wires into and among buildings on the campus. The radio signals "leak" from the wires and can be picked up by regular radio receivers located in close proximity without the need to be attached to the distribution system. Another unique feature of this type of college radio service is that it may carry advertising; the other categories, as already noted, operate under noncommercial licenses.

Ostensibly in response to several inquiries from carrier current college stations for permission to extend their coverage beyond the campus, the FCC, on April 4, 1971, issued a questionnaire to all college radio stations operating in the carrier current service. The questions included a request for information regarding news and editorial policy, financing, and distribution of revenues.

Again, the dissenter was Commissioner Nicholas Johnson. Among his reasons were the nearly complete absence of complaints regarding campus radio stations, the fact that the questionnaires were not restricted to stations that were requesting permission to go off-campus but were sent to all carrier current college stations, and the fact that there was evidence of political intent in the investigation. In circulating the original materials on this subject among the commissioners, members of the FCC staff had added an appendix containing articles from *Newsweek* (May 18, 1970) and *Parade* (May 31, 1970) that warned of the political content of college media broadcasts. The commissioners were again stampeded by the Pentagon, an interaction potentially as dangerous to establishment media as it is to underground media.

The commissioners supporting the inquiry joined in a rather ingenuous statement which began: "Campus radio [should] grow and add diversity to our method and content of information. [We] hope college students could appreciate our awareness of their growing importance."

The absence of deliberative judgment in these matters is apparent from the fact that the FCC did not have to launch a federal investigation to obtain the information it desired. The Corporation For Public Broadcasting (CPB) had released a comprehensive study of this subject just 18 months earlier.

The CPB survey found that most college radio stations obtain the bulk of their financing from student activity funds. The average budget ranges between $16,000 a year for carrier current stations to $47,000 for the high-powered non-commercial college stations. Only the carrier current services had advertising income. The average station earned about $5,300 a year from these advertisements. To aid them in obtaining commercial revenue, the carrier current stations are serviced by a number of national sales representatives such as the National Student Marketing Corporation, Campus Media, Inc., and Rock Media, Inc.

The CPB study also reported that college radio stations are an important training ground for the broadcasting industry. It was found, for example, that the college stations lose most of their staff members in their junior and senior years to local commercial broadcasting stations. A tabulation based on a subsample of 63 of the responding colleges showed that, as a group, about 900 of their graduates enter the broadcasting profession each year.

Absorption

The underground media have not only provided a means of expression for radical and disenchanted youth, they have evolved into the experimental proving ground for the next generation of journalists, editors and publishers.

Even before these young people have taken their place in the establishment, their techniques and their views have begun to appear in the establishment media. Many of the major media, broadcasting as well as print, subscribe to the underground news services, and some establishment journalists contribute articles to the underground press, generally under assumed names.

The adult community has accepted the youth culture's clothing styles, hair sytles, vocabulary, and its artistic and musical tastes. In addition, a significant number of planks from the underground's social and political platform have gained wide support and some have found expression in state and federal legislation. These include public policy in ecology and food safety, discontinuation of the military draft, reduction in the minimum voting age, and disengagement from the Vietnam War.

Most of these issues, though championed by the movement, did not originate with it. Rachel Carson's book, *The Silent Spring*, conservation groups, outspoken staff members of the Federal Food and Drug Administration, and network television provided the major impetus in making the public aware of the problems surrounding the quality of our environment and the purity of our food and water. Similarly, major advances in civil rights were achieved in the first half of the 1960's before the youth rebellion began. Nor can Kate Millett, Germaine Greer, or their sisters in the feminist movement be described as members of the youth culture. The anti-war movement in its early stages, the use of drugs by white middle class youth, experiments in communal living, and unstructured school programs are the principal planks in the underground platform that are more distinctly their own.

It is the toleration and partial acceptance by the adult community of many of the movement's views that constitutes the principal external threat to the future of the underground media, and to the youth culture. The ability to shock is reduced with time and exposure. And as the views, life style, appearance, and values which they advocate gain acceptance, their uniqueness and eccentricity are eroded. Evidence of the demise of the "movement" is the return of college youth to old fashioned antics, such as "streaking."

By incorporating eccentricity into the system, the establishment renders the eccentric predictable and, therefore, acceptable. Kate Millett, Abbie Hoffman, and Allen Ginsberg have now become part of the entertainment world. Their image in the public mind is that of an actor playing a role. Eventually, their identity as professional eccentrics replaced their ideas. As a sign of the times, Allen Ginsberg shaved off his beard and cut his hair. He did this just as sideburns and long hair made their appearance among the "hard hats" and in the halls of Congress.

It is also interesting to observe that the counterculture was not monolithic. The different groups constituting the "movement" advocated objectives that were often at cross-purposes. Thus black women wanted to have the experience of staying at home and being supported by their husbands while white wives strove for the reverse. Homosexuals demanded the right to be married and to be drafted into the military service, while young straights rejected both institutions. The anti-war groups stressed the sanctity of life while the same white middle class suburbanites and their radicalized youngsters advocated free and uncontrolled abortion. In the final analysis, freedom of the press survived the hostility of young radicals. But, as we shall see in the ensuing discussion it is not entirely certain that it will survive the well intended tampering of the establishment.

VIII

The Entertaining
Medium

The Task Facing Management

The programming demands placed on television are probably
beyond its capacity to meet. TV is expected to be all things
to all men. It serves as a supplement and sometimes even a
substitute for movies, newspapers, novels, magazines, the
theater, the town meeting, and the local school system.
Moreover, it has to appeal to all levels of sophistication and
taste. Its stories are expected to have the mass appeal of the
old dime novel and the sophisticated plotting of *The Spy
Who Came In from the Cold*. Its talk shows must possess the
fascination of the old gossip columns and at the same time
have the redeeming value of group therapy. The children's
programs must replace an older generation's *Perils of Pauline*
while coming to the rescue of the local school system. Its
news coverage is expected to combine the comprehensiveness
of the *New York Times* with the intimacy of a small town
weekly. This is no mean feat. Indeed it is virtually impossible.

Today's radio broadcasters have managed to get around similar demands in part by limiting themselves to a specific format such as soul music, or classical music, or simply news and weather. But they have mainly passed the buck to television.

Television programs, however, are costly—too costly to be effectively produced even by a group owner. Only by showing programs to the combined audiences of a hundred or more television stations, as the networks do through their affiliates, can the cost of expensive talent, staging, taping, and selling to advertisers, be made into a profitable business. The *size* of the audience is what counts and here lies the root of nearly all criticism of television programming.

Television's critics argue that one need not sacrifice quality for popularity. And, of course, it is true that some children's programs that edify also manage to keep the child's attention. *Sesame Street* has proven that. For the most part, however, audience surveys show that, even among adults, good solid drama, in-depth news programs, and sophisticated entertainment do not attract the largest audiences.

As an example, a half-hour program entitled *Escalation in Vietnam*, broadcast over the CBS Network on Tuesday, May 9, 1972 at 10:30 p.m. attracted only 25 percent of the viewing audience, while a rerun of *Marcus Welby, M.D.* broadcast by the ABC Network at the same time captured 41 percent of the viewing audience. Even the evening news broadcasts of all three networks combined attract, on the average, only one out of three households. Indeed, as a group, "informative" programs such as news, documentaries, discussions and interviews *at best* attract half as many viewers as a mystery, western, comedy or variety show.[1]

This reality has created a growing and potentially dangerous tension between educated viewers and those who operate the television communications system. The educated, who are articulate and influential, are pressing for some restraint on the profit motive so that the medium will serve their tastes as well as those of the "mass man."

As a compromise Congress created the Corporation for Public Broadcasting in 1967 and funds it annually (see Chapter X). For their part the commercial broadcasters are only too happy to have the intellectual market spun off, so to speak, if that means that there will be less objection to their own program fare. The high purchasing power of the educated has no special appeal for television advertisers. The sales appeal of soaps, beer, gasoline, deodorants, razor blades, dog food, and breakfast foods depends not so much on income as on age and sex.

Critics at Large

The attacks on network programming that hurt TV most come from 18- to 49-year-old women, the housewives and homemakers. They are the very core of the mass audience. They are the buyers of the products advertised on television. Their objection, however, is not to adult program fare but to what is and what is not being broadcast for their children.

An international survey of television programming shows that the United States is the only major country whose networks carry no weekday afternoon programs for children. At best, some local television stations run absurd and violent cartoons for the juvenile market.

Only the United States and Finland, according to another study undertaken by the National Citizens Committee For Broadcasting, confine children's shows principally to Saturday mornings. Also, children's shows carry 16 minutes of commercials per hour, twice the number carried on adult programs.

Although still a proposal rather than a rule, the FCC is now considering eliminating commercials from *all* children's programs and *requiring* 14 hours of children's programming each week.

The advertisers that would be most affected by a ban on children's commercials at the network level include: Kellogg, which spends $8.9 million a year; Mattel Toys ($7.8 million); and General Mills ($7.1 million). Together, these three corporations account for 25 percent of all children's advertising. Five other corporations, General Foods ($6 million), Deluxe Topper ($4 million), Quaker Oats ($3.8 million), Miles Laboratories ($2.6 million), and Mars, Inc., ($2.3 million) account for an additional 25 percent. These eight corporations account for over half of the three networks' total revenue received for children's programs. In all, about 80 companies advertise on children's network programs.[2]

Under ordinary circumstances this proposal would be too radical for serious consideration. But times have changed. For a number of years the FCC considered what seemed an even more radical notion: proscribing the number of hours during which the networks could broadcast and restricting their sale of television reruns in the secondary market (syndication). But this became a rule in 1971. And the total ban on cigarette commercials on radio and television which started in January 1971, is another "wild idea" that became a reality. Under the circumstances the FCC's proposal regarding children's programming seems less like an idle threat than it would have some years earlier.

Where did these proposals originate? Surprisingly, it was the Westinghouse Corporation that first suggested limiting the networks' use of prime time. The attack on cigarette commercials was initiated by John Banzhof, a New York attorney. A group of Boston housewives calling itself Action for Children's Television (ACT) advanced the 1970 proposal regarding children's programming, and the United Church of Christ successfully reversed an FCC decision to renew the license of station WLBT-TV on the precedent-setting grounds that the station ignored the local black population.

As we see, the principal advocates of greater government involvement in mass communications are public interest groups, and in one instance a major corporation. These are all members of the establishment, not members of a radical counterculture. The objectives of these and other public interest groups are well intended and for the most part, unselfish. It is for these reasons that they are successful and, unfortunately, why they are such a serious threat to the future freedom of our system of mass communications. After all, how can private interests desirous of protecting their profits oppose such lofty goals as health, racial equality, education of our children, and the improvement of adult entertainment?

But the profits earned in mass communication are the results of the media's ability to satisfy the demands of the majority. Public interest groups rarely represent the majority view in communications matters. Their goals must therefore be imposed by the government with all that this means for the freedom of the press, a concern that exceeds in importance all the altruistic goals of public interest groups.

One of the central complaints underlying the protests of many public interest groups is the alleged unchanging character of television programming. It is their belief that government intervention is necessary to foster change. However, television programming has changed radically over the years. The problem is that these changes have not been in the direction that they would have wished. The changes that have taken place were the result of technological developments and the accompanying expansion of the audience. In effect, television in America had metamorphosed into the nation's principal mass medium.

Evolution of Television Programming

In its early days television was a local medium. The American Telephone and Telegraph Company, which provides the facilities that tie together hundreds of affiliated broadcasting stations into networks, had not completed construction of even the basic relay or "backbone" system until 1953. During this early period most television programs were locally produced and live, or they consisted of old movies.

While AT&T's transcontinental video relay system was being expanded, network programs were transmitted live from studios in New York City. During this period the gross revenue of the networks increased from only $55 million in 1950, before transcontinental interconnection, to $233 million in 1953 after the first trunk line was completed. Twenty years later with a fully developed network system, the gross revenue (before commissions) of the three networks exceed $1.7 billion.[3]

The creation of a nationwide network of affiliated stations attracted national advertisers and provided the means of spreading the cost of programs, particularly of filming, among a large number of stations. The use of filmed programs permitted the director greater flexibility in the use of both indoor and outdoor settings. In economic terms it provided the producer with the potential of future resale, generally referred to in the trade as *syndication.* At that time, there was a large market for reruns of the evening shows in the daytime hours since in these early days the networks provided little daytime programming. Nascent foreign television services also came to rely on the American networks for low-priced syndicated programs.

When the telephone company finally completed its nationwide video transmission system, north and south as well as east and west, it consisted of 96,000 channel miles of intercity relays connecting 400 commercial television stations in 217 cities. During the final phases of its construction between 1953 and 1959, the number of television receivers in the United States doubled from 27 million to 55 million. This brought television into nearly 85 percent of the homes in the nation and supported a greatly expanded network schedule.

The character of the programming changed to meet the tastes of this mass audience. The wealthy and the educated were among the first to possess television. But as the price of television sets declined, the audience grew and its average level of education and wealth declined. The result was predictable: a gradual phasing out of the Sunday afternoon cultural schedule and the discontinuance of such programs as *See It Now, The Voice of Firestone, Omnibus,* and a whole genre of program known as the television play which for a number of years had been the dominant form of television entertainment. The talents that once wrote television plays— Reginald Rose, Rod Serling, Paddy Chayefsky and others— left the medium to become prominent contributors to the stage and screen.

The directors of television plays were also newcomers who have since left television and made their mark in another medium. John Frankenheimer directed the original television play "The Days of Wine and Roses" for *Playhouse 90* on October 2, 1958, at the age of 28. Since he has left television he has directed such films as *The Manchurian Candidate, Grand Prix* and *The Fixer*. Others of this caliber who worked in television in its early days and who have left the medium include Arthur Penn (*The Miracle Worker* and *Bonnie and Clyde*), Norman Jewison (*In the Heat of the Night, The Russians Are Coming, Fiddler on the Roof*), Franklin

Schaffner (*Planet of the Apes*), Sidney Lumet (*The Pawn-broker*) and others.

These talented artists complained that television had gradually evolved from the experimental medium it was in the 1950s into a tightly run commercial operation that was merely an extension of advertising. They also criticized the committee system, in which creative output was reviewed by business committees. This is the same criticism that used to be leveled at the movies when that medium was in the hands of the big studios. However, now that the movie industry is no longer a leading mass medium, *it* attracts the youthful experimenters and has become the status medium of the gifted.

Thus, the process of change has been present in television programming from the start, and without government prodding. The direction of this change, however, has been away from the lofty, the enduring, and the profound as television sought to bring pleasure to the mass audience. Public interest groups, almost by definition, are unsympathetic to mass tastes.

As technological changes converted television from an elite medium to a mass medium, its programming focused more and more on detective, espionage, adventure and cowboy subjects as well as situation comedy series with their canned laughter. Movies made especially for television were introduced in the late 1960s. They are generally lengthy pilots that may or may not turn into a series. It is a way of recouping some of the staggering sums invested in pilot programs. But special television films have yet to approach the quality of the early television plays. They more closely resemble lengthy versions of the standard western or detective series that are now basic television fare. In effect, the old dime novel is being presented on television in a number of different formats.

Program Turnover and Strategy

The sensitivity of television programming to popular tastes is most apparent in the turnover of television programming. *Broadcasting* magazine made a survey of the programs televised during the 1971-72 season, the first under the FCC rule limiting the networks to three of the four prime time hours (7 P.M. - 11 P.M.). As a result of this rule the three networks only provided 66 programs that season, or 15 fewer than the preceding year. Of these 66 programs, the survey found that 25 programs were *new*. Of the 41 "old" programs, only three survived from the 1950s: *Gunsmoke* (CBS), introduced in 1955; *Walt Disney* (NBC), introduced in 1954; and *Bonanza* (NBC), introduced in 1959. Twenty-eight programs survived through the 1960s but six of these were movie programs. Thus excluding the movies, only 22 of the 66 programs on the air in the fall of 1971 survived the 1960s (see Table 11). In effect, over 40 percent of the programs on the air that season were being shown for the first time. This rate of turnover is not at all unusual for television.

Now, the principal factor determining the survival of a network show is the relative size of its audience. And for this information, the advertisers and the networks rely on the audience measurements of the A.C. Nielsen Company. Reliance on audience ratings is analogous to maintaining a perpetual opinion poll regarding network programming and responding to the majority in determining the network schedule.

Popularity with the audience and quality as defined by "experts" are often mutually exclusive. Thus the 1970 winner of the National Academy of Television Arts and Sciences award for the best comedy series, *My World And Welcome To It* (NBC), disappeared from the network

TABLE 11

*Age of Network Television Shows
on the Air in Prime Time—1971-72*
Three Networks Combined

YEAR PROGRAM FIRST INTRODUCED	NO. OF PROGRAMS
New 1972	25
1971	3
1970	7
1969	9
1968	6
1967	3
1966	2
1965	3
1964	2
1963	0
1962	1
1961	1
1960	1
1950s	3
Total No. of Programs	66

Source: *Broadcasting Magazine*

schedule the following season. The determining factor in the network decision was the program's relatively low audience rating (percentage of homes tuned-in).

In more recent years, television audience research has involved, in addition to the rating, an increasing concern for the demographic characteristics of the viewing audience, specifically their age and sex. Does this portend a greater interest in subaudiences? If programming for such subaudiences should replace the present goal of programming for the majority, then women 18 to 49 years of age would probably become the main target of network programs since they are the major spenders for those types of goods that lend themselves to nationwide advertising. A shift of this sort, however, could increase the number of persons unhappy with television programming since the tastes of sub-groups differ sharply from the aggregate mass audience. In 1972, for example, at least six (one-third) of the eighteen most popular programs for the entire audience, failed to appear among the eighteen most popular programs listed for women 18 to 49 years of age. Among the shows that would have been axed, if the latter rating had been followed, were *Gunsmoke*, *Bonanza*, *Arnie*, *Mary Tyler Moore*, and *Adam 12*, the shows that were most popular with the general public at that time.

Of course a failing program is not always dropped. Sometimes, if the program's poor performance is attributed to another network's exceptionally popular offering, it is shifted to another time slot. If, however, the competition's offerings are also relatively unpopular, the decision is usually made to drop the failing program entirely. Such decisions are made periodically throughout the season. New shows are generally waiting in the wings, should an existing show fail to attract an adequate audience. To see just how such decisions are arrived at consider Table 12 which lists the results of a routine program review made by each network after the 1970-71 season had been underway for about 8 weeks. Note that the Table focuses on new programs, those that had been aired for the first time that season. The *rating* shown in the Table refers to the average percentage of homes in the nation that viewed the program, while the *share* refers to the proportion of all the homes *watching* television that viewed the program. If a program has a low *rating* but a high *share* it means that though the TV audience was small, that particular program obtained a dominant proportion of the audience, small as it was. NBC, for example, canceled *Nancy*, which obtained a rating of 17.7 while retaining *Four In One*, which had a lower rating of 17.0. The reason? *Nancy* had a share of only 28, while *Four In One*, had a share of 31.[4]

These decisions are made on the basis of an overall game

TABLE 12
Program Performance
and Network Decisions

PROGRAM	RATING	SHARE	NETWORK DECISION
ABC			
Barefoot in the Park	13.3	20	Cancelled
Dan August	11.8	21	Moved to 9:30-10:30 Thurs.
Danny Thomas	17.7	29	Moved to 9-9:30 Thurs.
Deadly Game	10.9	19	Cancelled
The Immortal	11.5	20	Cancelled
Matt Lincoln	11.9	20	Cancelled
Odd Couple	13.3	21	Unchanged
Partridge Family	17.0	30	Unchanged
Pro Football (Mon.)	17.8	30	Ends Dec. 14
Silent Force	13.5	21	Cancelled
Young Lawyers	11.5	19	Moved to 10-11 Wed.
Young Rebels	12.7	23	Cancelled
CBS			
Arnie	18.6	31	Unchanged
Headmaster	17.6	32	New format/same time
Interns	15.4	30	Unchanged
Mary Tyler Moore	20.7	35	Unchanged
Storefront Lawyers	15.8	27	New format/same time
Tim Conway	12.7	23	Cancelled
NBC			
Don Knotts	15.3	25	Moved to 8-9 p.m. Tues.
Flip Wilson	25.7	43	Unchanged
Four In One	17.0	31	Unchanged
Nancy	17.7	28	Cancelled

Source: *Broadcasting Magazine* December 21, 1970, p. 44.

plan. Network programming resembles a game of chess in which "counter-programming" and "audience flow" constitute the major strategies. Counter-programming means placing shows that are totally different from competing network programs opposite one another. Audience flow strategy, on the other hand, capitalizes on the general reluctance of television viewers to change channels. It seeks to capture the audience early in the evening and then to provide them with a sequence of programs that will not lead them to shift to another channel. In practice, this has resulted in evenings of very similar types of programs. In 1970-71, for example, NBC's Monday night schedule consisted of three comedies starting at 7:30 pm with *My World and Welcome To It*, followed by *The Red Skelton Show*, the *Rowan and Martin Laugh In* and ending with the Monday night movie. If you liked comedy you stayed with NBC all evening.

Using a counter-program strategy, ABC offered a series of adventure-excitement programs that same night. Its Monday night began with *It Takes A Thief*, which it replaced with *The Young Lawyers*, followed by *The Silent Force*, and then *Movie of the Week.*

Cost of TV Programs

The television networks spend more money to produce a single hour of *Gunsmoke*, *Columbo*, or *Marcus Welby, M.D.* than the average television station earns, after taxes, in an entire year. In 1973, one hour episodes of these popular series averaged between $200,000 and $225,000. And these are not the most costly television programs. The two hour movies shown on prime time television cost the networks about $325,000 an hour. NFL football cost ABC about $654,000 a game, or about $327,000 an hour. True, there are a number of programs that cost only between $90,000 and $100,000 an episode, but such episodes last only a half-hour. In effect even these cheaper programs cost the equivalent of $180,000 an hour.

Each of the three television networks spend an average of about $5 million *a week*, for programming, ranging from ABC's $4,800,000 to NBC's $5,400,000. And this cost keeps rising. Between 1960 and 1970 the cost of producing a one-hour network program had climbed by about 100 percent. *Broadcasting* magazine analyzed this substantial cost increase in a special report on one of television's longest run hits, *Bonanza*.[5] Produced by a crew of 34 and an NBC staff of 7, *Bonanza* did not enlarge its staff during its ten years, but the average cost of producing *Bonanza* increased from $114,000 for a one hour episode in 1960, to $211,500 in 1970 (see Table 13).

What accounts for this rise? Highly skilled specialists contributed much to *Bonanza*'s popularity. But skilled craftsmen are expensive. During the decade of the 1960s, hourly union wages of cameramen rose from $14.73 to $19.86; of makeup artists from $5.57 to $8.01; of prop masters from $4.43 to $6.54, and so on.

Other cost increases affected such diverse items as lumber, up 80 percent over the decade; animals, livestock and wranglers up from $1,315 per program in 1960 to $2,000 in 1970. The cost of space rented by NBC at Paramount Studios rose from $9,500 an episode in 1960 to $13,550 per episode in 1970. Even the coffee breaks for the production crew rose from $250 an episode in 1960 to $400 in 1970.

Then there are the stars of the program. Lorne Greene, Dan Blocker, and Michael Landon were all virtually unknown in 1960, and received $1,250 per episode in the series' first year. But by 1970 they each received $14,000 an episode and together accounted for nearly half of the program's talent cost. (The other talent categories include the script writer, music director, supervisers, the general cast and the guest star.) At the beginning top guest stars of *Bonanza* were paid $7,500 per performance. This was considerably above the

TABLE 13

Bonanza (NBC)

*Change in the Cost of Producing a
One Hour Episode by Item* *

	1960	1970
Supervision	$ 6,300	$ 22,990
Casts	18,000	55,885
Scripts	4,700	7,750
Music	5,000	5,850
Other	2,700	5,530
Total Above-The-Line	$ 36,700	$ 98,005
Production Staff	2,154	3,053
Camera	333	5,379
Extras	1,507	7,196
Set Operations	3,200	6,869
Electrical	3,558	6,276
Scenery	5,248	4,479
Sound	3,924	6,310
Makeup, Wardrobe	2,137	4,199
Props	3,247	5,722
Editing	3,691	8,704
Film & Lab	19,620	17,314
Transportation	750	1,511
Studio Facilities	9,500	13,550
Payroll Fringe Benefits	4,923	9,891
Miscellaneous	11,508	13,077
Total Below-The-Line	$ 77,300	$113,530
Grand Total	$114,000	$211,535

*Average Weekly Budget

Source: *Broadcasting Magazine,* Sept. 22, 1969, p. 62.

$4,000 that other filmed hours were paying at the time. Paradoxically, this is one of the cost items that declined and guests on *Bonanza* now receive $4,000 a performance.

It took four seasons for *Bonanza* to become profitable. Since then NBC has paid out over $52 million to produce this show. It now has a backlog of over 400 episodes, all in color, and it first went into domestic syndication in late 1972, which means that it will be around for some time. *Bonanza* is also seen abroad in 89 countries, including most of Western Europe and the Middle East, and parts of Africa, Latin America, and Asia.

Syndication

The cost of a television program is recouped by the producer from two sources: its lease to a network or broadcasters (who in turn derive income from the advertising that accompanies its showing) and the resale of the program after its first run. The sale of reruns is called *syndication*. The producer of the program has nothing to do with advertising, which we discuss in some detail in the next chapter. The sale of a program's reruns—its syndication—is where the program producer generally makes his profit.

But some programs cannot be sold for reruns. This is so not because there isn't a market for them, but because their "residuals"—that is, the fee received by actors or participants each time their program is shown—are too high. This fee has no relation to the price charged for the program on its resale, nor to the number of buyers, nor the success or failure of each customer in obtaining advertising to accompany the program's second showing. The "residual" is a fixed obligation, part of an original contract under which the talent was hired.

A single show of a variety program like the *Ed Sullivan Show* has so many different performers that the residuals are prohibitively high. This is why the immense backlog of decades of *Ed Sullivan Shows* will probably never be rerun. A single one-hour program that might have cost $155,000 for the original showing could cost, on rerun, as much as $50,000 for the residuals alone. Programs, moreover, are not sold one at a time, but for a season of several weeks. Thus a 13-week package in which each hour had a residual of $50,000 involves a $650,000 commitment on this one expense item alone. And these residuals will have to be paid for the *entire* package regardless of whether one or one hundred stations buy it.

As Table 14 shows, the average price for a one hour episode sold to a television station in one of the nation's ten largest cities is only $665 and drops to about $90 for cities ranking from 51st down to 100th in population. If the residuals run as high as $50,000, they cannot be recouped in the syndication market, and the residuals are only part of the cost in marketing a rerun.

The high risk of syndication explains why some independent producers, when they signed a contract with a network for a new series, preferred to relinquish all rights to a show's future earnings in return for a guarantee covering production costs plus a percentage for profits. On the other hand, if an independent producer believed he had a show that would

TABLE 14
Average Price Per Episode
Paid by Station for Syndicated Series—1968

| | ONE HOUR EPISODES | | | |
| MARKETS RANKED (BY POPULATION) | FIRST RUN | | OFF-NETWORK | |
	NUMBER SOLD	AVERAGE PRICE PAID	NUMBER SOLD	AVERAGE PRICE PAID
1 - 10	—	$—	14	$655
11 - 50	24	369	58	155
51 - 100	29	196	52	90
101 - 150	9	69	30	70
Over 150	2	88	11	37

Source: FCC Docket 12782/A. D. Little & Co. (1969).

hold up for more than one season, it was worth his while to try to hold on to the rights even if this meant losing money initially. Some production companies have been able to survive on the returns from reruns of shows like *Bewitched* and *Father Knows Best*. This type of show incurs much lower residuals than the variety programs. A $190,000 per hour series with just one or two principals in the cast would incur residuals of about $7,500 an hour. At this price, the marketing of the series is more manageable.

Figures on the syndication industry are not prepared by a central source. They emerge from time to time from special presentations to the FCC, as when the government proposed to eliminate network participation in syndication, a policy that took effect in October 1971. Estimates made at that time showed that in 1970 syndication sales totaled about $270 million—$170 million for domestic and $100 million for international sales.

All in all, about 80 percent of the networks' regularly scheduled prime time programming is eventually available for syndication. However, as the networks expand their broadcast schedules, the television stations have fewer time slots in which to run syndicated programs. In recent years network schedules have been expanded from seven to ten hours a day. True, the shrinking syndication market among affiliated stations is somewhat offset by the growing number of unaffiliated stations, currently numbering about 90. However, most of the unaffiliated stations lack the financial resources necessary for them to become a major market for syndicated programs. Before long, old programs may be less a sales problem than a storage problem.

Several rules-of-thumb apply to this field: It takes two to three years on the network for a show to pay for itself and to start clearing a profit for the producer. If a series doesn't hold up that long, syndication is its last chance to make money. If the show, when it is syndicated, isn't sold in New York, Chicago, and Los Angeles, it probably won't pay its residual costs and therefore can't make it in the secondary market. On the other hand, a show that doesn't make it for at least three years on the network is at a disadvantage, since it has proven that it possesses little appeal. Thus, the best guarantee of successful syndication is a long network run.

If at First You Don't Succeed

Since the networks command the gateway to the nation's prime-time television audience through affiliate agreements with three-quarters of the nation's television stations, it has been widely believed that they have to be accommodated if a program producer is to get his program on the air. This has led some critics to assume that, if only this monopoly could be broken, there would be a flurry of creative programming by independent producers.

The myth was put to the test in October 1971 when, following complaints from the Westinghouse Corporation which wanted to expand its television program production activities, the FCC freed one of the four prime time hours, *daily*, from the network-affiliate contract and prohibited the networks from selling syndicated programs or first-run programs for that time-slot. As already noted, however, this ruling did not achieve its stated objective of stimulating worthwhile production from non-network sources, and by 1974 the FCC was considering rescinding the rule.

A second aspect of this policy was a ban on the television networks' participation in the syndication market in general. Before 1971 the networks shared in much of the income from reruns. The FCC felt that this inhibited the entry of new producers who might otherwise be tempted by the additional source of revenue. Since the networks generally commission or underwrite—but do not own—the programs shown on television, the FCC's rule, in effect, keeps them from participating in the profits (and losses) resulting from programs produced by others. While, on the face of it, this seems like an equitable alteration in the marketing of television programs it very likely had the reverse effect. Since the costs and risks in this business are extremely high it was desirable from the producers' standpoint to have the option to shift the risk to the networks by letting them gamble on recouping their investment in the program from the reruns. Since the FCC ban, however, this risk must either be included in the base price or absorbed entirely by the producer. Considering that a television pilot program costs, on the average, about $375,000, this is not a very attractive alternative.

Thus, the FCC tried two approaches to reduce the role of the networks in television programming: it banned them from one-quarter of prime time and it banned them from the syndication market. The stated objective in each case was to stimulate new entrants into the business of program production but the implicit objective was to alter the character of the nation's television programs. Yet a viewing of current programs does not indicate any change in their basic character since 1971.

What the FCC failed to appreciate is that television is not *controlled* from the New York network boardrooms, but rather from Chicago, where the A.C. Neilsen Company tabulates the results of their on-going survey of the nation's television audience. As we shall see in the next chapter, the economic structure of the television broadcasting industry is such that maximum rewards are obtained when the largest possible number of persons are tuned in. The industry's executives are not confused as to their basic objective, and this guideline will necessarily result in the same type of programming regardless of who follows it.

IX

Advertising

The Hostile Mood

America's mass communication system is financed entirely by advertising revenue. This has freed the mass media from having to rely upon the government for financial support. Despite this critical role there has developed of late a strong and increasingly influential opposition to advertising which threatens to erode the media's economic base. This would open the door to government financing and thus, implicitly, to its involvement in the internal affairs of the mass media.

Disclosures at Congressional hearings that most breakfast foods are nutritionally valueless, that cigarettes are a health hazard, and that 15 percent of the drugs sold over-the-counter are of no use, have caused government regulators to call for restrictive legislation. But the restrictions being called for are not on the production and distribution of the offending products, but on their advertisement. More perplexing still, these critics are not even concerned about the advertising of these products in general, but only with regard to their being advertised on television.

Robert Pitofsky, Director of the Federal Trade Commission's (FTC) Consumer Protection Bureau, lists four major concerns of the agency: (1) advertising to children; (2) TV advertising that may "unfairly exploit desires, fears, and anxieties"; (3) TV commercials whose technical aspects of preparation "may facilitate deception"; and (4) the consumers' "physical, emotional, and psychological responses to advertising."

It should be noted that Pitofsky is not interested in deceptions that appear in print but only those that are televised. As Gerald Thain, also of the FTC has stated, "advertising practices that are tolerable in print have become intolerable today because they are on television and TV's impact is much more *powerful*." Here we have another example of the effect of communications mythology on public policy.

Senator Frank Moss (D-Utah), Chairman of the Commerce Committee's Consumer Subcommittee, wholeheartedly supports this approach. In 1971 he introduced a bill (S-1753) that would establish a "National Institute of Marketing, Advertising, and Society" that would be funded with $5 million. The Institute, he said, would gather knowledge of the social role of advertising and provide insights "to maintain advertising on *socially constructive paths*" (italics mine).

The momentum behind the trend toward government controls is increasing and will be hard to resist. The advocates of greater consumer protection do not believe that the common law, the courts, and the Pure Food and Drug Act are sufficient. They are calling for specific controls and regulations, some of which would involve the government in the details of advertising policy.

We have already witnessed the banning of cigarette advertising from radio and television although the product not only continues to be sold legally and advertised in the print media but tobacco growing continues to be subsidized by the government. Recent court decisions have given public interest groups the right to *free* air time for the purpose of attacking advertised products. As for the future, we have already noted that the FCC is now studying proposals to ban the televised advertising of drugs and the banning of all televised advertising aimed at children.

In dollar terms the cost of these proposals for the communications industry are so formidable that they represent a serious threat to the future viability of the mass media. For example, the ban on cigarette advertising over radio and television, in force since January 1971, involved a loss in advertising revenue of about $225 million a year.[1] In this case the loss was eventually made up by advertising feminine hygiene products and pet foods. However, the several proposals now under consideration by Congress, the courts, and the regulatory agencies, are so substantial that they are not likely to be offset by new commercial products. If so, the economic impact, particularly upon television, would be considerable.

Banning the advertising of drugs, for example, would cost the television broadcasting industry about $238 million a year. A ban on all advertising on children's programs would reduce revenues another $75 million a year. And if, as proposed, the FCC requires the industry to set aside an additional 14 hours a week for ad-free children's programs this would cost the industry about $424 million a year.[2] Together these three restrictions and requirements would cost the television broadcasting industry approximately $737 million a year in lost revenue. However, in 1972 the industry earned profits (before taxes) of $525 million.[3] Thus the projected losses stemming from current proposals would exceed total profits by one-third. Obviously this is an impossible situation.

Where did this hostility to advertising originate? It takes considerably more than a few "disclosures" by a handful of witnesses at a Congressional hearing to generate the kind of reaction that is being exhibited by the government and by public interest groups. There must have been a predisposition to the policies that have been adopted and those that are now being considered. It is suggested that this attitude rests on two broad issues: first the well founded belief that it is because of advertising that television programming is of the type that it is. That to obtain the largest possible audiences for the benefit of the advertisers, the public is offered what interests it most rather than what is thought "best" for it. And second, that many believe advertising to be a disreputable institution. This belief is based on a number of complaints regarding alleged advertising practices.

Thus it is claimed that advertisers regularly impose their own views on the entertainment and news that they sponsor. It is also claimed that the media who profit from advertising—especially television—fail to direct enough of this wealth into the type of programming that is in the "public interest." This is viewed as particularly irritating since the television medium has free use of the public's airwaves. And, as already noted, there is a strong feeling that advertisers mislead the public with regard to their products and in many instances, that they create wasteful and unnecessary consumption.

Clearly, with such a lengthy bill of indictment it would not take more than a few "disclosures" to set in motion a wave of "reform." Is advertising a corrupting influence? Is it possible that government support of the mass media might be a better alternative? Let us take a closer look at these allegations.

The Mythology of Advertising

Whether or not it was true in the past that advertisers, for private objectives, influenced the content of the programs they sponsored or the editorial policy of the newspapers in which they advertised, it is not true today. Today's advertising practices and the present economic structure of the industry have made it extremely difficult for an advertiser to exert such power upon the media.

In most major markets the absence of competing dailies of major size provides the principal local newspaper—and not the advertiser—with monopoly-like power. Newspaper revenues are derived from numerous merchants none of whose expenditures are critical for the survival of today's newspaper giants. Of the 2,300 retailers who advertise in the *Washington Post*, for example, only 20 spend as much as $100,000 a year; the biggest spends $3 million. Contrast that with the newspaper's gross revenue, which exceeds $77 million,[4] and we find that the large advertisers are more dependent on the major local newspaper than the other way around. Thus the multiplicity of local advertisers gives newspaper publishers in the United States independence not only from the government but also from any single advertiser.

In broadcasting, as we shall see, the advertiser no longer supplies the radio or television program, he merely purchases a few seconds each in various programs. Most programs carry the advertisements of a number of different companies, which effectively precludes any one of them from interfering with the material being broadcast. Furthermore, the largest single advertiser on network television, the Proctor & Gamble Corporation, spent only $116 million for network advertising in 1972.[5] Compared with the networks' gross revenue of $1.6 billion, this was only about 7 percent of the networks' total revenue. The greater dependence of P&G on access to the television audience than the networks' dependence upon P&G's advertising expenditures makes it very doubtful that P&G can exercise any power over the medium. Then, of course, the conflicting interests of P&G's competitors, both within the soap industry and among other product advertisers, makes the exercise of such power a candidate for our catalog of myths about mass communications.

Perhaps more important, network advertisers account for less than half of the industry's advertising revenue. The larger part, as discussed in some detail later, is obtained from the "spot" market and from local advertisers. At these levels there is not the slightest possibility of exerting pressure upon the medium to alter the content of the programs shown since these are all taped or filmed by independent producers for nationwide distribution. It is not technically feasible for a local broadcaster to regularly insert or remove scenes or comments from programs that he leases for local showing, or in one that is coming through the interconnection facilities of the networks. What the local broadcaster can do is refuse to carry a network show or refuse to lease a program from the syndication market. But when this is done it is to appease the tastes and biases of the local audience—with the encouragement of the government—and not in response to an advertiser's commercial or political interests.

Another myth is that television broadcasting, more than any other industry, can *afford* to be more public spirited and that its use of the public airwaves places the industry in debt to the commonweal. However, a great many industries use publicly financed or publicly owned facilities. This is true of the trucking industry, which uses tax-supported highways; the airlines, which use publicly financed airports; the farming sector, which is heavily subsidized with public funds; and the petroleum industry, which enjoys special tax privileges.

The other notion, that television broadcasting is unusually

profitable is not supported by the evidence. While it is true that in 1972 there were 133 television broadcasting stations (accounting for 21 percent of the industry) that were earning profits in excess of $1 million before taxes, it is equally true that there were another 158 television stations (25 percent of the industry) that were operating at a loss. Nearly half of the industry was somewhere in the middle, not losing money, but earning less than $1 million *before* taxes. Only 15 stations were in the charmed circle earning truly impressive profits. These earned profits before taxes in excess of $5 million *each.*[6]

We can get a better perspective of the profitability of the industry if we compare the profits of the entire television broadcasting industry, including the three television networks (ABC, CBS, NBC), with the earnings of individual industrial corporations. Table 15 reveals that in 1972 there were 13 industrial companies that *each* earned more profits than the entire television broadcasting *industry*. Similarly, in the service and trade sectors of the economy, eight insurance companies, a retail company (Sears Roebuck), as well as two utilities (AT&T and GT&E) *each* earned more profits than the entire television broadcasting industry in 1972.[7]

All in all, while the television broadcasting industry can boast of a few examples of fantastic profits among its television broadcasting stations, the industry as a whole does not stand out as particularly profitable, certainly not enough to suggest that it is its duty—more than that of any other industry—to finance the so called "public interest," which is in reality a euphemism for special programming for special interests.

There is another, a more important consideration. It is a mistake to look upon television and other mass media as simply another industry. Economic threats to the unhindered freedom of the mass media—implied in the demands for more

TABLE 15

Comparative Profits*—1972
(In Millions of Dollars)

General Motors	$2,163
Standard Oil (N.J.)	1,532
IBM	1,279
Texaco	889
Ford Motors	870
Mobil Oil	574
Standard Oil (Calif.)	547
Eastman Kodak	546
ITT	483
Du Pont	415
Standard Oil (Indiana)	375
Western Electric	283
Proctor & Gamble	276
Television Broadcasting Industry (incl. networks)	*276*

*After taxes

Sources: **Fortune Magazine** May 1973 and FCC Release 05693

public interest programming—could very easily rebound to the public's greater loss, should they result in a mass communications industry beholden to the government for its economic well-being. At that point an important part of the American political system, which depends upon continuous public scrutiny and surveillance of government, will have been rendered inoperable.

Deception Is Assumed

The third argument, noted above, underlying current hostility toward advertising, is the feeling that it is all too frequently deceptive and misleading.

Among the classic deceptions disclosed by the media themselves is the Colgate-Palmolive commerical which purported to show sandpaper being shaved using its Rapid Shave Cream. In fact, the sand was mounted on plexiglass since real sandpaper would have had to be soaked over an hour in the shaving cream in order to come clean. Then there is the case of Libby-Owens-Ford, which televised an open window to show the clarity of its glass. General Electric advertised its 10-inch color television set as "only half the price of many color sets"—its 10-inch set sold for $197. However, GE's 25-inch console sold for $499. "The latter," testified a straightfaced GE executive "is obviously more than twice as expensive."

Then there are the low-keyed deceptions consisting of such ambiguous slogans as:

"99 and 44/100 percent pure."—(Pure what?)
"There's nothing like (product)."—(Maybe that's a good thing)
"(Product) as only (company) makes it."—(Maybe that's a good thing too)

Actually, the public is far less naïve regarding advertising claims than the current concern of consumer protection groups and government agencies would lead one to believe. The number of products and political candidates that have failed despite well-planned and well-financed campaigns is legion. In addition to a natural skepticism, the public is frequently entertained by public and private exposure of just such advertising deceptions. These exposés, as already noted, generally appear in the very media that benefit from advertising.

As a matter of fact, few of the slogans, product endorsements, and demonstrations are really intended to convince the consumer of a product's superiority. Rather they attempt to establish public familiarity with a brand of a product that is usually bought casually, such as soap, cereal, or coffee. For well established brands, the ads seek to associate them with and "image" or state of mind like wealth, status, virility, or good times. In this context, deceptiveness in advertising is relatively inconsequential, if not meaningless.

In most mass-marketed items it is easy to shift from one brand to another, for the products do not last long. Hence, even the most flagrant deceptions are not a serious social problem. On the other hand, items that are expensive and that last long are much more likely to be closely inspected by a prospective purchaser. Whatever glowing descriptions may be published in advertisements regarding houses, expensive clothing, automobiles, and the like, they are almost always tested by the purchaser's own observation and inspection.

The current feeling that advertising should be more truthful if not actually informative reflects a fundamental misunderstanding regarding its function. In part, this can be traced to the changing character of the advertising profession.

In the last two decades advertising expenditures have increased enormously, doubling in each decade. There has also been a parallel growth in the size of advertising agencies. Several have even gone public and are now listed on the stock exchanges. The result is a widely held belief that advertising is an industry, indeed a growth industry. From this follows a fundamental misconception: that ads are products of this industry and that they, therefore, should be truthful in the same way that one would expect recently purchased food to be fresh or recently purchased appliances to be in good operating condition. Advertising, however, is not the product of a special industry, nor can advertising be an objective source of consumer information. It is merely old-fashioned salesmanship on a mass scale and it is as much an integral part

of the manufacturer's operations as is his shipping department. Its point of view, therefore, is *necessarily* biased.

No company can realistically be expected to spend large
sums of money to criticize or be "objective" about its own
product. By its very nature, advertising deals in half-truths. It
proclaims the favorable aspects of the product and is silent
about the less favorable. This is a common practice in many
walks of life. It is done when applying for a job, when
preparing for a date, and when campaigning for political
office, as well as when selling goods and services.

Advertising *harmful* products is not the issue, for in such
circumstances it is not the advertisement that should be
discontinued but rather the production and distribution of
the product. Harmfulness aside, it is naïve to expect
producers to bare their souls by confessing a competitor's
advantages or their own inadequacies when selling an otherwise useful product.

Creating Wants

Another common complaint against advertising is that it
sometimes causes people to purchase products they do not
really need. To the extent that this is true, (and this is not as
easy as assumed) it amounts to a very pleasant type of tax.
These purchases ultimately support the mass media by
encouraging advertising expenditures. The alternative would
be government support of the media, which would also be
obtained through taxation—but of the unpleasant type. More
important, and an aspect of government support we must
never forget—is that it inevitably entails a constraint on our
freedom of expression and on the availability of information.

This "expansion of wants" has another side to it. Classical

economics assumed that there was an automatic demand for the output of industry—that the problem was simply one of bringing price and quantity into equilibrium. But this has proven to be unrealistic. Because of the immense productive capacity of modern industry the consumer has to be induced to desire the goods and services he can produce in his role as a worker. Otherwise they pile up on the shelves and unemployment ensues. Advertising has become a particularly important link between mass production and mass consumption.

The Advertiser in Search of an Audience: Media Analysis

The image of the advertiser as a mind bender, possessing awesome power over the behavior of his audience, is a myth founded on the public's unfamiliarity with the processes involved. In fact, advertising is a highly risky business. Millions are spent in a single advertising campaign without the slightest knowledge, until considerably later, as to how many people even saw the advertisement, much less whether it was successful in terms of the advertiser's sales volume. It is much like fishing. You can bait the hook with the best lure and use the finest equipment, but unless you have chosen the right spot and the right time there might not be any fish in the area. And fishermen know well that even then, "they may not be biting."

Thus advertising involves a perpetual search for the most efficient method to reach just those persons who are prospective customers. There is an implicit acknowledgment that a customer can rarely be made out of whole cloth. The prospective buyer is understood to be in the market looking for the product and the principal task of advertising is to induce that prospective buyer to purchase the brand being advertised.

In selecting media, the advertiser's objective is to reach the maximum number of the right people, with the right frequency, and in the right mood or atmosphere (movies aren't advertised on the obituary page), for the lowest cost per thousand prospects.

Most media attract fairly well-defined audiences. Thus the audience of a local newspaper or television station is defined by its geographical location. Magazines designed for men or women define their audience by sex. Even programs on radio and television are able to offer advertisers access to fairly well-defined audiences. Sports events (males); soap operas (female homemakers); cartoons (children); and rock music (teenagers) are all programs directed at sub-audiences.

The advertiser also has to determine the probability that his advertisement will be seen. There are studies of "page traffic" in newspapers for example, which show that the front page is read by 99 percent of readers while the back pages reach only 25 percent or 30 percent. Yet this 25 percent readership can be more significant than the 99 percent if the advertiser is selling to a specific audience. To reach men he will use the sports section, to reach women he will use the food or fashion section. An independent research study by Daniel Yankelovich undertaken for 30 newspaper markets revealed that as many as 80 percent of the women who read newspapers read the food section regularly, not occasionally.

The Cost of Advertising

It generally comes as a surprise to those unfamiliar with the processes involved that the advertiser knows what he is spending, but not what it is costing. The reason is that he has a budget for advertising so that he knows his dollar expenditures, but not until long after the ad or commercial has been released is he aware of the size of the audience that saw or heard his message. Thus he doesn't know whether he paid $2 or $8 to reach a thousand prospective customers.

If the public rejects the program carrying his commercial the advertiser takes a loss in the form of wasted advertising expenditures. If the program catches on or retains an already established popularity, he has been successful. In either case there is no certainty, and the risks can be very high. Table 16 shows the network price for 30 second commercials offered to advertisers six months before the 1971-72 season began. A purchase of just two such spots for a thirteen week season can exceed $1 million. And this does not include the cost of creating the commercial itself.

Because of the risks involved there are few sponsor-owned programs on the air today. Instead, as noted earlier, the networks buy or produce the program and then sell participating ads to several advertisers. This permits the advertisers to spread their risk by buying time in a number of different programs.

The cost of air time is only part of the price paid for

TABLE 16

Television: Price of 30 Second Commercials—1971-1972

	WINTER	SPRING	SUMMER
Flip Wilson	$43,000	$31,000	$21,000
Nichols	64,000	50,000	42,000
Gunsmoke	34,000	34,000	20,000
Arnie	25,000	24,000	18,000
Marcus Welby	42,000	35,000	30,000
The Odd Couple	26,000	20,000	17,000
Movie of the Week	32,000	23,000	20,000
Carol Burnett	29,000	28,000	17,000

Source: *Broadcasting Magazine* April 5, 1971

advertising on television, though it is the greater part of the cost. The other cost component is the commercial itself. In 1968 the American Association of Advertising Agencies submitted, as part of an experiment, 17 commercials that had been made in 1963 for rebidding at a number of film houses. None of the film houses knew that they were participating in a survey or that the commercials had been produced before. A comparison of 1963 costs with 1968 bids revealed an average increase in production costs of 72 percent.[8]

One important factor in the increased cost of television commercials is the use of color. Not only is the raw film itself more costly, but color requires a longer shooting day, more emphasis on makeup and wardrobe and more precision in lighting.

During the same 1963-68 period the price of television air-time also increased. It climbed 73 percent at WCBS in New York City, the nation's largest market and 84 percent at WHAS in Louisville, Kentucky, a relatively small market. But the *real* cost increase was somewhat lower than that, since during this period the number of television homes reached by these stations had increased by 13 percent in New York City and by 28 percent in Louisville. Thus the net cost of air-time increased about 64 percent in New York City and 61 percent in Louisville. Of course, this is in addition to the 72 percent average increase in producing the commercial itself. In the last five years, these costs have undoubtedly increased even more sharply.

Another significant myth concerning advertising and the mass media involves the belief that large advertisers receive substantial discounts to the disadvantage of their smaller competitors. In the early days of television the networks sold only air-time to advertisers who themselves supplied the programs. Under this type of arrangement there were volume discounts. But the discounts were only for the purchase of air-time, the programs were purchased by the advertiser directly from the program's producer. This was a carry-over from the radio network days. These discounts posed some serious anti-trust problems and were the subject of more than one Supreme Court ruling.

However this issue has ceased to be a matter of concern with the rearrangement of business relationships. For many reasons, some already discussed—including the rising cost of programming, the change from live programs to film and tape, the increasing length of programs and the increased risks involved—advertisers today no longer supply their own programs, but purchase time in programs supplied by the networks. Under this new arrangement referred to as "participations," there are no volume discounts by any of the networks.

The price of "participations" is usually finely tuned to the estimated value of the size and type of audience generated by a given program. These prices change quite frequently in response to changes in general market conditions and in audience characteristics.

Varying prices are quoted for "participations" in the same program, but, as shown in Table 16 these variations, are for different seasons of the year in accordance with the audience's viewing patterns. Price lists are made widely available to the trade and the same prices are offered to all advertisers, regardless of size. If these listed prices are not validated in the market place—if the audience isn't what was expected—bargaining ensues and new prices are established. At intervals new lists are prepared, reflecting both general market conditions and changes in the market's evaluation of individual programs, based principally on audience surveys.

While television's advertising rates were skyrocketing, the cost of newspaper advertising increased only slightly. Thus in the same period discussed above, between 1963 and 1968, the *millne rate* (cost of an agate line per million copies) increased on the average only 9 percent, from $3.95 to $4.30. The increase since 1968 has been at an equally slow rate. The reason for this relatively slow rise in the cost of newspaper advertising can be attributed to the relative stability in operating costs faced by newspapers, the presence of alternative modes of reaching local consumers, and the predictable nature of the local market.

It is interesting to note that in the newspaper field, it is frequently the giant national companies that pay a premium for advertising rather than the relatively small local businesses. Those firms who use the newspaper medium infrequently are charged 60 percent over and above the price paid by local advertisers who contract for newspaper advertising by the year. For this reason national advertisers prefer to employ "co-op" advertising, where they share the advertising costs of the local merchant, thereby benefiting from the deep discounts he receives from the local press. By 1970, co-op advertising totaled $1.5 billion paid to retailers, who themselves put a total of $2.7 billion into newspapers. Department stores led the list with $800 million in newspaper advertising of which $430 million came from "co-op" funds spent by national manufacturers.

Another unique feature of newspaper advertising is the classified ad. Today nearly 30 percent of all newspaper advertising revenue (about $2.3 billion) comes from this source. And its importance is growing. In the last decade the value of classified advertising increased by 85 percent.

The Structure of Advertising

Today advertising accounts for approximately 75 percent of the revenue received by newspapers, the rest of their revenue comes from the sale of the newspaper itself. In the case of commercial radio and television, advertising provides nearly 100 percent of the revenue received. In return, advertisers receive 60 percent of all newspaper space (up from 40 percent in 1940) and about 17 percent of prime-time television (7:00 P.M.-11:00 P.M.). In non prime-time the Broadcasters' Code allocates to advertisers up to 26 percent of television time. As for radio, the Broadcasters' Code recommends that advertising not exceed 18 minutes per hour or 30 percent of air-time. However, less than half of the radio stations in the country have agreed to be bound by the provisions of this voluntary code.

Improvements in mass communication have vastly accelerated the growth of advertising. Back in 1935, when even radio was in its infancy and the nation suffered from economic depression *total* advertising expenditures in the United States were only $1.7 billion. By 1951 this sum had quadrupled. By 1960, when television was reaching into nearly 90 percent of the nation's homes, all forms of advertising in the United States totaled $12 billion. A decade later it exceeded $25 billion, of which the mass media accounted for over half.

Following the second world war, all forms of mass media were put to use to sell the vastly expanded output of the nation's farms and factories. Thus, contrary to widespread predictions, the boom in television did not doom radio but paralleled a period of unprecedented growth in radio broadcasting. Radio's advertising revenue actually doubled in the decade of 1959-1969. This same period also witnessed an unprecedented growth of advertising in newspapers and magazines.

As shown in Table 17, newspaper revenues from advertising are growing even more rapidly than those of television. Available data show that between 1969 and 1973 newspaper revenues—excluding revenues received from subscriptions—

TABLE 17

Trend of Advertising Revenue
(Billions of Dollars)

YEAR	TOTAL	NEWSPAPERS	TV	RADIO	MAGAZINES
1973*	$15.0	$7.7	$4.3	$1.5	$1.5
1969	12.1	5.8	3.6	1.3	1.4
1959	6.5	3.5	1.5	.6	.9
1949	3.0	1.9	—	.6	.5
1939	1.2	.8	—	.2	.2

*Estimated

Source: *Advertising Age* August 27, 1973. Prepared by McCann-Erickson, Inc.

increased by 32 percent while television's advertising revenues increased by about 20 percent.

Aggregate data on advertising revenue do not, of course, explain significant differences in the economic function of the different mass media. Thus advertising consists of two basic markets—local and national. The local advertising market is the larger of the two. In 1972, as shown below, the local advertiser—which includes department stores, chain stores, supermarkets, automobile dealers and classified columns—together spent $7.9 billion on advertising. This was 30 percent more than the advertising expenditures of national advertisers using the mass media. In dollar terms the local advertisers spent $1.8 billion more than national advertisers.

As shown in Table 18, the principal medium for *local* advertising is the daily newspaper which receives 74 percent of all such expenditures. Radio actually outperforms television in the local market. For *national* advertising the principal medium is television, which received about half of all national advertising expenditures. Magazines rank as the second most important national advertising medium.

TABLE 18

Sources of Advertising Revenue—1972
(Millions of Dollars)

MEDIUM	NATIONAL		LOCAL	
Newspapers	$1,103	18%	$5,905	74%
Television	3,112	51	960	12
Radio	475	8	1,080	14
Magazines	1,440	23	—	—
Total	$6,130	100%	$7,945	100%

Source: *Advertising Age* August 27, 1973. Prepared by McCann-Erickson, Inc.

On Socially Constructive Paths

Advertising, as we have seen, is a complex institution of considerably greater importance than is generally recognized. Yet, private groups and public agencies today advocate government rules that would limit and regulate its activities. They are particularly intent upon reducing the interdependence between advertising and mass communication. This may be motivated, in part, by a lack of knowledge regarding the delicate market mechanisms that permit advertising to serve as the economic base of mass media in the United States. Unfortunately, there is more to this problem.

Reformers today have managed to wrap themselves in a cloak of sanctity that a previous age had reserved for clerics and theologians. In the process they have created an intellectual environment that has imposed a litany of unquestionable premises upon matters of social, political and economic importance. Thus the belief that if one's aims are unselfish they are necessarily desirable, is all too frequently the basis of the most questionable schemes "in the public interest."

How can anyone argue in favor of a self-serving institution such as advertising? In today's intellectual climate it is not only unfashionable and in bad taste, it is considered antisocial. Yet the truth of the matter is that the results of the policies advocated by public interest groups and government agencies in the field of advertising and mass communications pose a very serious threat to our political freedom.

In advocating control over advertising one is saying, in effect, that the public must be protected from the purveyor of goods. Yet the Constitution protects the purveyor of ideas. It does this on the assumption that the public is able to judge for itself what is good and what is bad—or more important, it assumes that no one else is better qualified to do so without causing greater harm in the process. It is a very small step, however, from the assumption that the public is economically naïve, to the assumption that it is politically naïve.

An example of the extreme to which our confidence in the public's good sense has taken us in noncommercial matters can be seen in a recent FCC ruling that refused to censor a white racist, J. B. Stoner, whose 30 second spot announcements over television and radio stations in Tennessee and Georgia could accurately be depicted as a very serious threat to the safety of our citizens. Stoner's "announcement" which the FCC did not consider to be a public menace is quoted here: "The main reason why niggers want integration is because niggers want our white women. I am for law and order with the knowledge that you can't have law and order and niggers too."

The complaint against this announcement was made by a broadcaster who argued that by compelling him by law to carry such an announcement, the FCC makes the public think that a broadcaster will publish anything for money.

The FCC required that he carry the announcement because

"the public interest is best served by permitting the expression of any views that do not involve a clear and present danger of serious substantive evil that arises from public inconvenience, annoyance, or unrest."[9]

It is difficult to see how one agency of government (FCC) exhibits such supreme confidence in the public's ability to absorb such a raw insult calmly (which with hindsight it in fact did) and another agency of government (FTC) show such lack of faith in the public's ability to ignore a questionable sales pitch for deodorants and shaving cream.

Some government agencies tend to overestimate their own wisdom and to underestimate the ability of individuals to discriminate among the many appeals made to them. What is needed today is a new sense of modesty about the abilities of government bureaucracies and an awareness of the destructive power they wield. The government, after all, can litigate endlessly. It matters little to the FTC that the final determination of a case may take one, two, three or more years as it goes through the full trial and appellate process. Yet such an ordeal of litigation can literally ruin an average business.

Today it is fashionable in some quarters to disdain advertising and indeed there is much in advertising that merits disdain. But to demand perfection as the price of survival is to make a demand that no one is even capable of defining. As the FTC itself noted in its decision in the Pfizer case (1971):

Unfairness is potentially a dynamic analytical tool capable of progressive evolving application which can keep pace with a rapidly changing economy. Thus as consumer products and marketing practices change in number, complexity, variety, and function, standards of fairness to the consumer also change.

Fairness aside, history has shown time and again, that however *crooked* a businessman or group of businessmen may be, the danger they represent to the public's welfare is but a fraction of the threat posed by a government that seeks to keep its citizens "on a socially constructive path."

It should be remembered that advertising revenue provides the means by which mass communications in the United States has secured its independence of thought and action. That is what makes the current trend toward increased government interference in advertising so disturbing. For what is ultimately at stake here is not the survival of advertising. What is at stake is our society's historical right to information completely free of government interference.

It may sound odd to associate liberty with commercial advertising but they are, in the final analysis, closely related.

Mass Media
in Mass Education

Relative Efficiency

The nation's educational system serves 60 million students from the primary grades through college. The cost of educating these students is estimated at about $86 billion a year which comes to about $1,433 per pupil. By comparison the mass communications industry spends about $15 billion annually. With this sum newspapers, radio, television and magazines serve approximately 220 million Americans. This is an average of about $68 for each member of the "audience."[1]

A large part of the very significant difference between the per pupil cost of formal education and the per person cost of informing and entertaining the public is the result of differences in technology. Formal education is still largely a personal process. Each class of students carries the cost of at least one teacher with supporting staff, the cost of school supplies, and its share of the cost of the school building, overhead, and in many cases, transportation. Keeping the public informed and entertained, on the other hand, is accomplished by means of sophisticated cost-reducing equipment, including intercontinental space satellites, microwave interconnected broadcasting stations, low-cost and long-lasting television receivers, transistorized radios, and high-speed presses.

There is also a very substantial difference in "reach." The educational establishment employs more than 3 million teachers, plus additional supporting staff, in order to reach 60 million students.[2] The mass communications industry, on the other hand, is able to serve 220 million people while employing only 485,000 persons in all its occupations. Thus the average reach per employee in mass communications is about 453 persons as compared to 20 students per teacher. Mass communications thus has a reach that is about 22 times greater than that of the educational system. This differential goes a long way toward explaining the difference in their cost per person reached—for education costs about 21 times more per person served than mass communications. Clearly, technology spells the difference. Can or should the technology of mass communications be applied to mass education? The question goes to the heart of the American approach to education, for here too we face the question—who controls these media?

The Principle of Diversity

Ethnic and cultural diversity has long been the distinguishing feature of American society. The desire to preserve this diversity and the fear of domination by any one group has historically prevented the centralization of mass education.

The identifiable geographic location of many ethnic groups (Swedes in Minneapolis, Irish in Boston, Poles in Pittsburgh, Italians in Providence) has also helped mold the character of the American educational system, with its division into 20,440 relatively autonomous school districts.[3]

The size and number of these districts vary widely among the states. Nevada, for example has 17 school districts while Nebraska has 2,013. There is a similar diversity with respect to financing. Thus Oregon raises 75 percent of its school funds locally while in Delaware school districts get only 20 percent of their money locally, the balance coming from the state. Educators from other Western countries continue to be amazed that such a diversified and autonomous school system works as well as it does.

Still, efficiencies and cost economies of mass communication present a great temptation to educators—and taxpayers. There has, as a result, been a decided drift toward the use of the latest communications technology in American education. This raises some serious questions. Will the techniques of mass communication when applied to mass education change the basic diversity of our school system? If so, what are the long range social and political implications? The answers to these questions are beyond the scope of this book. But an awareness of the forces that control the electronic instructional media is a necessary first step in evaluating their impact.

Public Television

Public television is aimed at a minority audience composed principally of people who wish to be informed as well as entertained. It is a multi-service medium that used to be called "educational" television. More recently it is referred to as "non-commercial" or "public" television since most of its revenues come from federal and state funds.

In 1967 Congress created the Corporation For Public Television (CPB) as the organization for channeling federal funds for the programming of numerous ETV stations then being licensed by the Federal Communications Commission. For a number of years the federal appropriations totalled about $30 million a year. Then, in 1973, Congress passed the first long-term appropriation, a two-year funding of $175 million plus another $55 million to assist in the development of physical plant. For the first time, public television could plan ahead for a number of years.

After years of fumbling a sorting-out has taken place. Instead of the locally produced shoe-string productions circulated for years by the National Association of Educational Broadcasters (NAEB) and the National Educational Network (NET), public broadcasting operations are becoming centralized. The NAEB tape library has been phased out, and the NET has become a production unit for station WNET in New York City rather than for the entire system.

In their place CPB, the new Corporation for Public Broadcasting, has designated seven of the more developed ETV stations—Boston, Washington, D.C., Pittsburgh, Chicago, San Francisco, Los Angeles, New York City, and the Southern Regional Network (SECA)—as production centers. These production centers are to be coordinated by professionals employed by the Public Broadcasting Service (PBS), the new operating arm of CPB. The PBS assigns the number of hours of programming and the type of programs to be produced at each of the eight production centers and sets the budget for these productions.

The structure of this organization (PBS) was carefully designed to insulate the programming process from political forces. Even so, it is unlikely that those government officials in control of the pursestrings will easily relinquish their power. And, in fact, in early 1973 the government did seek to place programming decisions under CPB, whose directors are White House appointees.

Another ominous sign is the conflict developing over the agreement that PBS signed with the Bell Telephone Company establishing a nationwide microwave system to interconnect all public broadcasting. This will, in effect, create a fourth nationwide television network out of the nation's 240 public broadcasting stations. At present this network does not include the instructional morning programs that are piped into many of the nation's school systems, and about which we will have more to say. However, if in the future those programs, too, are "networked" the principle of decentralized education in the United States will undergo severe strain.

Our concern in this chapter is not with the growth of a fourth network for *general* programming shown in the evening. As we see in Table 19, the type of programming offered by public television in the evening, is an important addition to the type of programming available from the commercial networks. Rather, our concern is with the very substantial block of time that public broadcasting stations devote to instructional television (ITV) in the morning. It is the instructional part of public television that poses a possible threat to the decentralized character of our educational system.

Instructional Television

On the average, educational television stations in this country carry about 21 hours of instructional programs (ITV) a week, which is equal to 28 percent of their air-time and accounts

TABLE 19

Comparison of Programs
Commercial and Public Television—1972

TYPE OF PROGRAM	PERCENT OF HOURS
COMMERCIAL NETWORKS	
Children's Programs	8.1%
News	12.4
Sports	9.3
Drama	11.8
Comedy	18.2
Daytime Serials	15.8
Feature Films	10.6
Quiz Shows	13.8
	100.0%
PUBLIC TELEVISION	
Children's Programs*	39.7%
Musical Performances	6.9
Nonmusical Performances	13.8
Cultural Programs	9.5
Public Affairs	30.1
	100.0%

*Includes instructional programs (28.1%)

Source: *One Week of Public Television* (CPB) May 1973, p. 24.

for 43 percent of their programming.[4] It is estimated that enough schools exploit this resource during school hours so that it now reaches approximately 23 million students, or about 40 percent of the total student body in the United States. In addition some 10 million students are exposed to educational radio as part of their in-school instruction.

It should be noted in passing that printed matter presents less of a problem. There are two widely distributed school newspapers, the *Weekly Reader* and the *Junior (Senior) Scholastic*, and of course there are school texts. These have generally been tailored to local desires. Unlike educational television and educational radio, the printed media do not contribute to centralization of education for they do not circumvent the classroom teacher. On the contrary, use of printed matter enhances the teacher's role, since she must be there to interpret its content. When using electronic media, however, the presence of a trained teacher is unnecessary; indeed it would defeat the whole purpose of efficiency and cost saving offered by a "master" teacher located in a distant production center and able to serve a wider audience. Clearly, the outmoding of the classroom teacher poses a serious problem.

Yet the trend toward "electronic education" is getting little publicity. The proliferation of equipment and facilities has enabled state and federal authorities to program mass education of American students with little thought for the future of America's traditionally local approach to education.

By 1972 the Public Television System in the United States comprised 240 stations with a potential audience equal to about 75 percent of the nation's population.[5] The ownership of these stations falls into four categories: stations owned by local communities, which account for 25 percent of those licensed by the FCC; stations owned by a state (35 percent); those owned by a local school district (11 percent); and stations owned by a university (29 percent).[6]

These stations when combined, accounted for only 32 percent of the instructional television programs produced, a sharp decline from the 56 percent they produced in 1964. The states produce about 6 percent and regional networks about 7 percent. The bulk of ITV programming today (55 percent) comes from *national* organizations. Also important to note, by 1972, about 15 percent of the ITV programs were distributed by interconnected microwave relay in much the same way as the entertainment programs of the commercial networks. The balance was "bicycled" around on video tapes or film.[7]

This situation will eventually come to a head when PBS or a sister group at the national level undertakes to produce ITV programs on a major scale. This is a genuine possibility, although currently PBS accounts for fewer than 5 percent of the ITV hours. Since more than half of the nation's ITV programming already comes from national organizations, they, like the producers of general programming, will eventually be taken under the wing of PBS. This would be consistent with the current trend toward consolidation.

Then, too, there is likely to be pressure for a more efficient use of the interconnection system of Public Television. If it is underused in the morning hours when ITV accounts for nearly all of the programming, it seems reasonable to expect that at some point use will be made of this facility to tie many of the 240 Public Television stations into a nationwide ITV network. By either route, or possibly both, we will have stumbled into a centralized, nationally directed educational system.

Education Through Commercial Television

Two kinds of educational programs are shown on commercial television: (1) documentaries, which are often on prime time on commercial television and then loaned in film or tape for use by closed circuit systems or Public Television stations; and (2) experimental college level instruction televised over commercial stations in the early morning hours.

Loans of documentaries to educational facilities by commercial television have made a very small impact upon the educational market. Public Television stations report that only 1.8 percent of their general programming and 0.3

percent of their ITV programming is obtained from commercial television.

As for instructional programming by commercial television, there have been only a limited number of experiments with college-level instruction on commercial broadcast stations. In 1958, a nationally televised college-level physics course, *Continental Classroom*, went on the air, underwritten by foundation grants and carried by more than 150 NBC outlets at 6:30 in the morning. In subsequent seasons courses in chemistry, math, and American government were also offered. Although more than 300 colleges cooperated in the program and viewing was said to be heavy, the program was dropped. Currently the program *Sunrise Semester* is seen in several major metropolitan areas, but it remains an isolated experiment. Other than these examples, there has been no substantial attempt to televise instructional programs on commercial television.

More recently the mounting protests of numerous groups against the present style of children's programming on commercial television has focused attention on this segment of the program market. To date, however, the educational role of commercial programming can only be described as incidental.

Educational Radio

Although they are junior partners in the use of mass communications for education, educational or non-commercial radio stations are much more numerous than their television counterpart. The latest count puts their number in excess of 450, or nearly twice that of Public Television stations.[8] But compared to the 5,100 commercial radio stations in the

United States, educational radio stations are few in number. In addition, many educational radio stations are insignificant. Thus, one-third of them have an effective range of only two to five miles. Such shortrange stations generally serve a college or university campus (see Table 20), which explains their ability to continue in operation despite their small audience (more often than not consisting of the school's dormitories).

TABLE 20

Ownership of Educational Radio—1970

OWNER	NUMBER OF STATIONS			
	FM	AM	TOTAL	% OF TOTAL
Colleges and Universities	228	16	244	70%
Public School Systems	50	1	51	15
Independent Schools	10	0	10	3
Bible Colleges	10	1	11	3
State Councils	10	1	11	3
Educational Organizations	13	0	13	4
Public Libraries	3	0	3	1
Municipally owned	2	1	3	1
Total	326	20	346	100%

Source: Herman W. Land Associates

Only one AM educational radio station is municipally owned (WNYC in New York City). The concept of community ownership simply does not exist in educational radio, as it does in educational television where 25 percent of the ETV stations are community owned, and 11 percent are owned by a school district.

Educational radio costs very little to operate. Almost half of the educational radio stations operate on less than $20,000 a year and only 14 percent spend more than $100,000 a year. The target audience of educational radio is the general public. But the programming is sometimes tailored to special groups. The largest specialized audience are college students as one would expect with colleges and universities owning about 70 percent of the stations.[9]

These stations get their programming wherever they can. There are several organizations for them to turn to, but unlike television, they have no plans for live interconnection.

Toward Consolidation

Contributing to the concern regarding future reliance on regional or national ITV for use in schools is the current trend toward administrative centralization in school districts across the United States, a trend that most educators agree will increase the overall efficiency of the system. In the fall of 1963, there were 31,700 public school districts in the United States. By 1973 consolidation had reduced that number to 20,300, a decrease of nearly 45 percent. If we go back to 1945, the decline appears even more startling, from 101,400 to the present 20,300. Clearly, the trend is toward more students in larger school districts.

Administrative centralization, however, should not be equated with standardization of curriculum. Indeed teachers, traditionally a key influence on children, have increased in number while the number of administrative units were decreasing. But if in the future a significant proportion of the learning process is shifted to ITV then the question of standardized curriculum becomes an issue.

In social and political matters, important changes are often wrought through innumerable small decisions. Such irreversible decisions are being taken now. Will it be in the public interest to trade off the present dispersion of authority over our educational system for a more efficient "machine"? Until the answer to this question is clearly established as a result of intensive study and thought, the current drift of events poses a very serious threat to traditional local control of our system of mass education.

XI

American Media Abroad

The AFRTS

The United States is not only the world's dominant user of mass communications; it is also a major supplier. In a field so sensitive that much of the world is prohibited by their governments from hearing or reading another nation's media, America's *private* producers annually sell abroad over $80 million in television programs, including news stories that account for as much as 20 percent of the information provided to much of Western Europe. American television producers supply West European television with nearly as many entertainment programs (other than sports) as does the European Broadcast Union.[1]

In addition to these private sources, about which we will have more to say later, the American *government* through the Defense and State Departments also exports programming. Thousands of American servicemen stationed abroad watch their favorite American television programs each night—minus the commercials. Few of them, however, realize the number of foreign nationals that are also listening to the international system of 300 radio stations and 61 television stations that constitute the Armed Forces Broadcast Services (AFRTS). In Europe alone, the Armed Forces' radio audience is conservatively estimated at 20 million civilians.

AFRTS had its start on July 4, 1943, in a BBC cellar. Originally designed to serve American Army units in the British Isles during World War II, its responsibilities were expanded as time went on. Its last reorganization, in August of 1967, placed it under the Office of Information of the Armed Forces, which reports to the Assistant Secretary of Defense for Manpower and Reserve Affairs. Its stations are staffed by both civilian and military personnel, with military officers usually serving as station managers. Civilians generally operate the programming and engineering departments.

The content of Armed Forces radio has been described as reminiscent of American radio before television. It includes packaged interview shows specially recorded in Los Angeles for AFRTS. Most stations, however, use U.S. radio network shows. They are frequently connected directly to the U.S. private networks through short-wave relay. Thus AFRTS picks up news and sports events at the same time that the civilian audiences receive them in the United States. On-the-hour news from all four major U.S. radio networks is used in rotation and local disc jockey shows provide all types of music during off-hours.

Television programming, on the other hand, is not carried live from the United States except on rare occasions. AFRTS TV stations carry standard U.S. fare, videotaped and shipped by air to the armed forces stations. News programs are assembled at each station from film clips flown in and from local sources.

The impact of Armed Forces Radio and Television on foreign civilians has not been measured by scientific audience research, since the informing and entertaining of foreign nationals abroad is not an officially recognized objective of the Department of Defense. Clearly, however, the knowledge that there are local audiences does affect programming decisions.

Military Censorship

The experience of AFRTS provides ample evidence that a government-operated communications system finds it virtually impossible to resist the temptation to censor the news. Defense officials say that there is little management of the news and that what there is is justified on grounds of military or national interest. But the facts say otherwise.

Thus, in the fall of 1969, the 11 radio stations and eight television stations operated by AFRTS in South Vietnam were ordered not to carry accounts of a public statement by South Vietnam's Vice President, Nguyen Cao Ky announcing a U.S. troop withdrawal. Instead, Americans in Vietnam had to read about it in the local English-language newspapers or the serviceman's own publication, *Stars and Stripes*. Nor did AFRTS listeners hear, until more than a week after it was broadcast and printed widely in the United States, that on one occasion a company of soldiers had refused to fight.

The central operating headquarters for all of AFRTS is in the Washington suburb of Rosslyn. But some orders to kill stories over the entire network have come directly from the nearby Pentagon. One such story concerned the 6,000 sheep killed by lethal nerve gas at the Utah Dugway Proving Ground in 1968. AFRTS newsmen in Washington also were told to delete stories concerning speculation that Spain might not renew its treaty permitting U.S. bases there. Ironically, another story killed was a report from a UPI reporter in

Saigon telling how AFRTS newsmen had charged, on-the-air, that their news was being censored.

Although an edict by former Defense Secretary Robert McNamara that "the censorship of news stories or broadcasts over such outlets as AFRTS is prohibited" is still in force, there is another Defense Department directive—also still in force—which allows information considered sensitive to the host country to be suppressed. Present and former employees of the service say the widest possible interpretation is given to this loophole to satisfy news management.

Beyond Censorship

Foreign interest in AFRTS is substantial precisely because it is not intended for foreign nationals. The foreign audience wants to know what America is telling its own people about different events. But the American government also operates a system of mass communication intended specifically for foreign audiences. These media were designed to meet the needs of an environment most Americans would not even begin to comprehend.

Control over information in the U.S.S.R. is so stringent that it is a criminal offense to own an unregistered typewriter. The 300 million people living in Eastern Europe and the U.S.S.R. are not only denied information that might reflect badly on the government but also information of commonplace events. Indeed they are even denied information regarding their own laws.[2] The authorities find it easier to violate their laws if the public is ignorant of them. The unlawful exile of the Nobel Prize author, Alexander Solzhenitsyn, is an example of but one of untold violations of the rights of Soviet citizens by their own government. It is the disclosure of these violations in his writings—almost all of which had to be published abroad—that eventually led to his exile. On the other hand, were it not for the fact that his reputation was made known in the U.S.S.R. by foreign broadcast media his very life would have been at stake for the crime of communicating information.

The American media beamed at Eastern Europe and the U.S.S.R. are not attempting to increase America's popularity. Rather their purpose is to serve as a surrogate free press for the people living in these closed societies. The motivation is not altruism but a realistic understanding of the importance of information. The $250 million a year spent on this effort is an attempt to limit the freedom of action of these totalitarian regimes. As noted earlier, information is the substance of power. By reducing the state's monopoly on information these media help to make the regime answerable, even in a limited way, to public opinion. Indeed many of the dissidents in the Soviet Union are alive today because their names and their alleged offenses were made known by these media, throughout Russia.

It was with this in mind that Radio Liberty serialized Solzhenitsyn's book, *Gulag Archipelago*, as soon as it was available in the winter of 1974. The possession of a recording or typed copy of *Gulag* is a criminal offense in the U.S.S.R. and for a good reason. This book's central theme is a factual account of the violence perpetrated by the Soviet regime on its own people, including the names of persons and details of actual events. Its threat to the regime is in an informed public.

The American media that are involved in these efforts include Radio Free Europe, which is beamed only at Eastern Europe, and Radio Liberty, which is beamed only at the U.S.S.R. The Voice of America also broadcasts into this region in addition to broadcasting to the rest of the world.

Significantly, the Soviet authorities have, since September 1973, eased their jamming of the Voice of America, but they continue to jam Radio Liberty. In this effort they employ approximately 3,000 transmitters at an annual cost of about $300 million.[3] The selective nature of Soviet jamming reflects differences in the policies of these independently operated—though Congressionally financed—media. Thus in early 1974 Russian dissidents complained that the VOA had curtailed its coverage of Soviet affairs to protect the detente. A survey of VOA programming confirmed that news of Soviet affairs had indeed been cut back considerably. This analysis of VOA programs showed that dissident news, political stories about domestic Soviet affairs, and the U.S. press opinion on Russia—a key item for Soviet listeners—had diminished by 61 percent. State Department officials deny that there has been a clandestine deal regarding VOA policy. But the results speak for themselves.

The VOA is part of the United States Information Agency (USIA) and accounts for about one-quarter of its budget, or $48 million a year. The USIA also operates a worldwide network of libraries and public information offices and sponsors international conferences. Much of its efforts are aimed at friendly countries.

Radio Free Europe (RFE) and Radio Liberty share a $45 million budget, of which Radio Liberty generally receives about one-third. RFE listeners number about 30 million people or nearly half of the adult population of Eastern Europe. The size of the audience listening to Radio Liberty is much more difficult to determine. There are fewer Soviet tourists traveling abroad than East Europeans, and Soviet tourists are more likely to be watched when they are abroad and therefore are more reluctant to be interviewed.[4] However, based on the best available information, Radio

Liberty estimates that it reaches about 15 percent of the Soviet population despite intensive jamming by the authorities.

The size of these audiences does not represent an accurate assessment of their impact. Information in an information starved country has a way of spreading that makes a simple count of initial listeners a poor basis for evaluation. There has been an instance when these media can take credit for affecting Soviet foreign policy. Thus, in 1968, a leading Soviet scientist, Andrei Sakharov, circulated a memorandum in which he urgently called for bilateral cooperation with the United States on matters of disarmament and environmental control. The SALT treaty and the Environmental Treaty signed five years later are traceable, at least in part, to the stimulus of Sakharov's memorandum. However, this memorandum was not published in Russia, it was broadcast back to Russia by Radio Liberty and the VOA.

Despite the importance of these media for the foreign policy of the United States there are some who propagate the myth that we are improperly interfering in the internal affairs of foreign nations. Among those fostering this myth is Senator J. W. Fulbright, Chairman of the Senate Foreign Relations Committee. However, the act of communicating to foreign nationals is a right that is enscribed in a number of international covenants. Thus, jamming of foreign radio broadcasts violates Article 19 of the United Nations Charter of Human Rights and Article 48 of the 1965 Montreux International Telecommunications Convention. The U.S.S.R. is a signatory of both, and takes full advantage of this freedom in *its* overseas broadcasts. Indeed the U.S.S.R. is second only to the United States in exercising that right (see Table 21).

TABLE 21

Sources of International Broadcasting *—1972*
Number of Hours Per Week *

U.S.S.R.[†]	2,090	
Eastern Europe	1,952	
China (People's Republic)	1,584	
		5,626
U.S.A.	2,193	
Western Europe	2,020	
		4,213
Others (selected)[‡]	1,739	
		1,739

*Represents the sum of different languages
†Includes 204 hours on clandestine radios
‡Portugal, Spain, Australia, India, Japan and Canada

Source: **Report Of The Presidential Commission On International Radio Broadcasting,** Government Printing Office, Washington, DC (1973).

Unofficial Influence: TV Syndication

As far as the free world is concerned the *official* American media such as AFRTS and the Voice of America, are relatively unimportant. The flow of *unofficial,* that is, commercial programming is the principal mode of communication between the United States and the rest of the world. Paradoxically our contact with the Communist countries is limited by their own governments to our official government media. If there was a free flow of information with the Communist countries there would be no need for the USIA, RFE or Radio Liberty.

The foreign market for American commercial television is considerable. More than 95 percent of all American television network programs are sold in at least one foreign country—mostly during the same season in which they are being shown in the United States.

American television programs are sold to about 100 countries and syndicated television news reaches about 40 countries. Canada, Australia, Japan, and Western Europe are the principal purchasers of American television programs. The prices they pay are based either on the popularity of the programs (number of viewers) or the number of TV sets licensed in those countries which require such licenses. Each half-hour of a popular series sold to Britain, for instance, sells for about $4,000, while a half-hour of the same program sold in Panama may bring only $50. Thus the revenue earned from the export of television programs understates the original cost of production and, inferentially, the number of foreign nationals exposed to American programming.

Initially, U.S. syndication grew at a rapid rate because the desire of other countries for programming outstripped their ability to produce. In addition, U.S. shows are priced to sell at much less than the production costs of foreign producers. Britain's Independent Television Authority estimated that they could buy a typical U.S. show for one-tenth of what it would cost them to produce it. But, in recent years, foreign governments, even friendly ones, have been less enthusiastic over the influx of U.S. programming. Britian, Australia, and Canada now prescribe a maximum percentage of programming which may be imported from the U.S. The quota for Australia, for instance, is 14 percent.

It is difficult to assess the impact of television shows exported by America. Some critics in this country worry about the image of America portrayed in some of the more popular programs which feature crime and violence. Others are concerned over the casual treatment of luxury in America for a world still full of poverty. Most critics feel that we need to be represented overseas by something more than the cliché formulas of cowboy serials, detective films and situation comedies. This concern is based on the myth of the public's credulity, a strain that runs through all media related issues. But a society in which information flows freely is not so easily misled. In Western Europe there is little likelihood that the American fiction shown on Europe's television screens will distort their public's understanding of American realities.

Our Printed Media Abroad

Programs for broadcasting are not the only form of information and entertainment exported by the United States. Approximately 18 million copies of U.S. newspapers and magazines are distributed abroad each month.

U.S. general interest magazines with international editions, which constitute the bulk of the 18 million copies sold abroad, are ranked in Table 22.

The *Reader's Digest* is by far the most widely circulated magazine in the world. It is published monthly in 30 separate editions. Both the text and the advertisements take into

TABLE 22

U.S. Magazines With Foreign Editions

MAGAZINE	TOTAL FOREIGN CIRCULATION
Reader's Digest	10,946,000
Life*	909,000
Time	823,000
Popular Mechanics	434,000
Newsweek	229,000

*Has suspended publication since survey.

consideration the cultural sensibilities of particular markets. Thus advocacy of birth control would not appear in the Irish edition nor would the sale of liquor be advocated in editions sent to Moslem countries.

Of U.S. newspapers with overseas circulation it is surprising that 73 percent of the total circulation is attributable to a U.S. Spanish language newspaper *Hablemos*, which is little known to most Americans.

Also included in the list in Table 24 is a newspaper not published in the U.S., but published specifically for Americans abroad, the *Rome Daily American*.

America's printed material has a smaller overseas audience than American television programs. Reliable audience figures for U.S. television programs shown abroad are not available, but they are certainly in excess of the 18 million that receive U.S. periodicals. However, if *readership* is projected at four times the circulation figure, the resulting 72 million is formidable, especially since it is concentrated in Western Europe.

U.S. periodicals are generally used by what American advertisers refer to as the "influentials"—people in a position to influence policy and style. Almost 10 percent of the 18 million circulation is accounted for by business, trade, technical, and scholarly journals. These journals necessarily influence the attitudes of foreign professionals, principally because the content of these publications is not frivolous entertainment nor propaganda, but truly informative and educational. Then too, American periodicals have generally reflected American society more realistically than have television programs. In a survey of TV viewers nearly 60 percent of the respondents did not believe that American life was really as portrayed in American TV programs. No magazine would long survive if its credibility were that low. This statistic also speaks volumes about the purported gullibility of the audience.

TABLE 23

U. S. Magazines
The Circulation Abroad of Regular Domestic Editions

MAGAZINE	TOTAL FOREIGN CIRCULATION	FOREIGN CIR. AS A % OF TOTAL CIRCULATION
National Geographic	361,000	9.09%
Playboy	325,000	9.75
Ladies Home Journal	76,000	1.17
McCall's	65,000	0.78
Scientific American	52,000	13.27
Esquire	45,000	5.02
Seventeen	45,000	3.49
House and Garden	42,000	3.01
Popular Photography	39,902	9.51

TABLE 24

U.S. Newspapers with Foreign Circulation

NEWSPAPER	FOREIGN CIRCULATION
Hablemos (Spanish)	474,000
Herald Tribune: European Ed.	80,000
Journal of Commerce	32,000
Rome Daily American	30,000
New York Daily News	16,000
Christian Science Monitor	14,000
Miami Herald	12,000
Wall Street Journal	2,000
Total	660,000

Epilogue

It would have been impossible to plan the American system of mass communications as it is now constituted. The variety of modes, concepts, functions and audiences, which make up the system defies imagination. What is even more startling is that this system evolved from the efforts of thousands of independent decision makers. Yet, as we have seen, it is a well balanced and efficient machine.

Entertainment, information, and advertising flow to the American audience in a great variety of print and broadcast packages. The audience is continually surveyed for its opinions and this information results in continual adjustment of media output. No other nation has a mass communications system so finely tuned to the desires of the audience it serves.

As discussed in some detail in this book, there is a clear link between the media's mode of operation and the fact that *no one* in mass communications in the United States is a government employee. The government is excluded by design from participating in the operation of the system. This arrangement, however, has now come under considerable pressure from forces outside of government as well as from the government itself. Currently this is a matter of major concern.

But America's mass communication system is rooted in the soil of commerce, not politics. Indeed there is not a single party network broadcasting station, or daily newspaper in the United States. The system is designed to fit into a consumer oriented economy. Originally, entertainment programs were intended to help sell radio and then television receivers. Gradually it evolved that these media were important instruments for the sale of other goods and services. Today they share with newspapers and magazines the important function of linking mass production to mass consumption.

We are now on the brink of another major change in mass communication. By the end of 1975, there will be more than 100 broadband channels in domestic satellites owned by half-a-dozen different U.S. corporations in orbit over the United States. Each channel can carry a video picture or alternatively several thousand voice conversations. Initially television will have to follow a circuitous and costly route to reach the nation's homes from these satellites. But the time is not far off when these satellites will be able to broadcast directly to the home. This technology is already in use abroad.

At that point, the process of creative destruction, discussed earlier, will have again been set in motion with a significant impact on television broadcasters and the television networks. In time there will be international use of satellites that broadcast direct to the homes of foreign nationals, much as radio does today. This could have immense impact on such closed societies as Russia, China and Eastern Europe.

As we have seen within the United States, there has been a decline in political bossism with the increased development of mass communication. This strongly suggests that the relentless exposure of persons and policies to the glare of public scrutiny exerts a force, not on the audience, but on those whom the audience observes.

It has been fashionable to bemoan the possibility of electing computer-primed "nonentities" to high office simply because of their public charm and the so-called power of the media. However, these observers would do well to look into the past and explain how such charming nonentities as Van Buren, Tyler, Fillmore, Pierce, Hayes, Harrision and Harding managed to become presidents of the United States. Indeed, it is possible that the relentless public exposure of modern communications would have prevented these lesser lights from attaining high office.

The mass media are like a time machine, they accelerate the process of familiarization, but this familiarity can just as easily breed contempt as popularity. A case in point is the late Senator Joseph McCarthy who terrorized the federal apparatus, but was destroyed by the image he projected on the television screen. Thus, it can be argued that the mass media are image *breakers* with at least as much conviction as the more popular belief that they are image *makers*.

The "power of the media" is a cliché to which reference is almost always made in discussion of this sort. This power has been accepted as real, yet it consists principally of the ability to reach a phenomenal number of people at the same time. If by power one also means the ability to influence, it still remains to be proved that man's ability to direct others has increased because of technology. The existence since the dawn of history of mass movements and totalitarian regimes indicates that political and social ills would still exist, with or without mass communications. One should not forget that Moses, Jesus, Mohammed, Confucius, Buddha, Marx, and Lenin, did not have the benefit of today's sophisticated technology and advertising budgets, yet their points-of-view and their personalities still command a great deal more attention than any of our contemporaries. Perhaps we have forgotten that the key to influencing people is, after all, ideas rather than technology.

Notes

CHAPTER I

1. Periodicals: *Editor & Publisher Yearbook* (New York: 1973).

    Television: *Nielsen Television Index* (Chicago: A. C. Nielsen Company, 1973).

    FCC Release 05693 (1973).

    Radio: FCC Release 92704 (1972).

    Weekly Papers and Magazines: *Ayer Directory of Newspapers and Periodicals* (Philadelphia: N.W. Ayer and Son, 1973).

2. Marshall McLuhan, *Understanding the Media — the Extension of Man* (New York: McGraw-Hill, 1964). Harry Crosby, *The McLuhan Explosion* (New York: American Book Co., 1968). Raymond Rosenthal, *McLuhan: Pro and Con* (New York: Funk & Wagnalls, 1968).

3. *New York Times*, February 18, 1973.

4. Erik Barnouw, *The Image Empire* (New York: Oxford University Press, 1970).

5. *New York Times*, January 26, 1973.

6. Broadcasting Magazine

7. *Special Study* (M. H. Seiden & Associates, 1969), FCC Docket 18110.

8. *Broadcasting Magazine*, June 21, 1971, p. 28.

CHAPTER II

1-3. Series of Senate Hearings on the Failing Newspaper Bill (1969-1970). *Subcommittee on Antitrust and Monopoly*, 90th Congress, 1st and 2nd sessions.

4. FCC Annual Financial Summaries.

5. Ibid.

6. *TV Factbook 1973-1974* (Washington, D.C.: TV Digest, Inc.) p. 76a.

7. Chris Welles, "Can Mass Magazines Survive?," *Columbia Journalism Review* (July/August, 1971) p. 7.

8. Ibid.

9. *Broadcasting Yearbook*, (Washington, D.C.: Broadcasting Publications, Inc., 1972).

10. L. F. Palmer, Jr., "The Black Press in Transition," *Columbia Journalism Review* (Spring 1970) p. 31.

11. *Ayer Directory of Newspapers and Periodicals* (Philadelphia: N. W. Ayer and Son, 1973).

12. *Time Magazine*, March 4, 1974, p. 38.

13. FCC Release 05693, Table 3 (1973).

14. Ibid.

15. *Fortune Magazine*, May 1973.

16. FCC Release 05693.

CHAPTER III

1. *Special Study* (M. H. Seiden & Associates, 1971), FCC Docket 18110. The basic data for this study were obtained from computer tapes through the sources listed below and were coordinated with supplementary up-to-date information available in the trade press. Each media owner was assigned an identification code which permitted the computer to coordinate the data from diverse sources relevant to all of his holdings. Where overlapping ownership existed, ownerships were combined, e.g., Cowles-Ridder, McCormick-Patterson. Television: American Research Bureau, Inc. Radio: Pulse Inc. Newspapers: Sinding, Inc. Weeklies: National Newspaper Representatives, Inc. Magazines: American Bureau of Circulation.

CHAPTER IV

1.   Newton N. Minow, John Bartlow Martin, Lee M. Mitchell, *Presidential Television* (New York: Basic Books, Inc., 1973) pp. vii-xi.

2.   Dale Minor, *The Information War* (New York: Hawthorne Books, 1970) p. 12.

3.   Marvin Barrett, ed., *Survey of Broadcast Journalism* (New York: Grosset & Dunlap, 1970) p. 33.

4.   *Washington Post*, November 1, 1970.

5.   Minow, Martin, Mitchell, *Presidential Television*, pp. vii-xi.

6.   Seiden, *Special Study.*

7.   FCC Report on Political Broadcasting (1973).

8.   *Ibid.* In 1972, the presidential campaign accounted for $14.3 million of the $59.3 million spent by all candidates for radio and television (network and station time). Senatorial races accounted for $6.4 million, Congressional races for $7.4 million, Gubernatorial races for $9.7 million, and all other state and local candidates spent $21.5 million.

CHAPTER V

1.   E. G. Krasnow, L. D. Longley, *The Politics of Broadcast Regulation* (New York: St. Martin's Press, 1973).

2.   *Broadcasting Magazine,* January 1, 1973; February 12, 1973, p. 24.

3.   Ibid., January 8, 1973, p. 16.

4.   *New York Times* Magazine Section, 1973.

5.   Ben Bagdikian, *The Information Machines* (New York: Harper & Row, 1971) p. 131.

6.   Martin H. Seiden, *Cable Television: USA* (New York: Praeger Publishers Inc., 1972).

7.   Bagdikian, *The Information Machines*, p. 70.

CHAPTER VI

1.   *Washington Post*, August 16, 1971.

2.   Ibid. March 30, 1971.

3.   David Zineman, "Should Newsmen Accept PR Prizes?," *Columbia Journalism Review*, (Spring, 1970).

4.   Leo Bogart, "Survey of Foreign Correspondents," *Journalism Quarterly* (Summer 1968).

5.   Julius Dusha, "Columnists and Pundits," *More*, Vol. 1, No. 2.

CHAPTER VII

1.   Caroline Meyer, "The Preteen Market," *Television*, July 1967, p. 37.

2.   Ibid., p. 27.

3.   *Nielsen Television Index* (Chicago: A.C. Nielsen Company).

4.   Robert J. Glessing, *The Underground Press* (Bloomington, Ind.: Indiana University Press, 1970).

5.   *Wall Street Journal*, August 13, 1970.

6.   FCC Release 71-205.

7.   FCC Release 71-428, p. 3, fn. 5.

CHAPTER VIII

1.   *Nielsen Television Ratings* (Chicago: A. C. Nielsen Company, 1972).

2.   *Broadcasting Magazine*, May 10, 1971, p. 17.

3.   FCC Annual Financial Reports.

4.   *Broadcasting Magazine*, December 21, 1970, p. 44.

5.   Ibid., September 22, 1969, p. 62.

CHAPTER IX

1.   *New York Times*, April 18, 1971.

2.   In the average television hour the television broadcasting industry as a whole earns $582,000 (1972). Multiplied by the annual total of 728 hours (14 x 52 weeks) that present proposals would have devoted to children's programming free of commercials, yields a loss of income of $424 million a year.

3.   FCC Release 05693, Table 3.

4.   *Washington Post*, August 19, 1971.

5.   *Advertising Age*, August 27, 1973.

6.   FCC Release 05693, Table 7.

7.   *Fortune Magazine*, May, 1973.

8.   Caroline Meyer, "War on the Cost of Making Commercials," *Television*, August, 1968.

9.   *Broadcasting Magazine*, August 7, 1972, p. 14.

CHAPTER X

1. *U.S. Statistical Abstract—1972*, p. 106, Table 156.

2. Ibid., p. 430, Table 674.

3. Ibid.

4. Nathan Katzman, *One Week of Public Television — April 1972* (Washington, D.C.: Corporation for Public Broadcasting, May 1973).

5. S. Young Lee, R. J. Pedone, *Summary Statistics of Public Television Licensees 1972* (Washington, D.C.: Corporation for Public Broadcasting, October 1972).

6. Ibid.

7. Ibid.

8. *Summary of Statistics of CPB Qualified Public Radio Stations 1971* (Washington, D.C.: U.S. Department of Health, Education, and Welfare, January 1973).

9. S. Young, R. J. Pedone, *Financial Statistics of Public Television Licensees 1971* (Washington, D.C.: Corporation for Public Broadcasting, October 1973).

CHAPTER XI

1. Based on discussions with principals.

2. H. Berman, *Justice in Russia*, (Cambridge: Harvard University Press, 1963) p. 76.

3. "Impediments to the Free Flow of Information in the USSR," *Radio Liberty* (November 20, 1972).

4. *Report of the Presidential Commission on International Broadcasting* (Washington, D.C.: Government Printing Office, 1973).

Index